What people are saying a

Already I can feel the change in my life . . .   Emily Brantley

Anil is extremely insightful . . . he has helped my family   Dr. Richard Castellano

I have found life more fulfilling   Ravi Bhanot

It was such a profound experience   Lina Moumni

Anil has changed the quality of my life measurably and
has added more years to life my life and more life to my years   Roger Salam

Got to the root of my problem immediately   Dr. Emile Allen

It was really awesome   Cindy Love

Anil has a gift   Bob Murray

He managed to resolve some of my issues in 10 minutes
that other people have taken years over   Andy Pancholi

The results were absolutely instantaneous   Shirley Hadley

It was absolutely phenomenal   Mark Hadley

Anil truly has a gift . . . unbelievable . . . numerous breakthroughs . . .   Mina Shah

Give you inner peace   Aladdin Kazran

I learned so much, it is absolutely life changing   Doris Young

I thought it was very inspiring   Nathalia Martinez (aged 10)

IMMEDIATE HAPPINESS

IMMEDIATE HAPPINESS

Be happy NOW using practical steps with immediate proven results

Anil Gupta

Book Cover Design by Verbii.com
Cover photo by Terri Zollinger, www.terrizphotography.com
Book Interior Layout by Sunny DiMartino

Printed in the United States of America

10 9 8 7 6 5 4 3 2 1

Library of Congress Cataloging-in-Publication Data
Gupta, Anil
Immediate Happiness
ISBN-13: 978-1-935989-03-5
ISBN-10: 1935989030

Summary: When you power yourself, you will empower your life.

1. Happiness 2. Self Help 3. Personal Transformation 4. Motivational 5. Self Esteem 6. Success 7. Mind and Body

This book works with Anil's Master You, Master Life Series. There are educational seminars, workshops, retreats and a DVD series available on this subject matter. For more information, please visit the following website:

www.immediatehappiness.com

CONTENTS

PART TWO

*Dedicated to my beautiful wife Meena
and our children Anu and Ajay.*

*May you all know the gratitude and love
I feel, each and every day.
You have blessed me in many ways.*

ACKNOWLEDGMENTS

It gives me the greatest of pleasures to dedicate this book to my beautiful bride, Meena Gupta, and a great friend, Scott Humphrey. It was during the most difficult times of my life that my wife, Meena and my friend Scott stepped up to help me. Together, they have coached, guided, and nurtured me. Without their help I really would not be in this position to help others. I owe my life to them. They were truly supportive in my hour of need. My worst day of my life became the best day of my life. This book has been written in my own words and with a pure, passionate and heartfelt desire to help you.

To Scott and Meena, I am your servant.

Thank you, so, so, so much for allowing me to help others.

FOREWORD

Anil is famous for creating immediate results in his transformational workshops and seminars. When searching for his work online, or meeting event or retreat participants, these are the types of things you will come across and hear:

"I have just attended Anil Gupta's seminar and the impact that it has had on my life, well, words cannot describe. The feeling that I have, the motivation that I have, to work on the relationships around me, to bless other people around me, with my family, with my boyfriend, with my school friends. Anil really knows what he's talking about and already I can feel the change in my life."

"I would like to basically say that it is absolutely amazing. We were able to use all the practical tools and basically anything that he was able to say to us and do for us, we were able to use it and apply it in our life."

"I have had the privilege of knowing Anil Gupta and he is amazing. He really has helped my life on many levels. He's helped my relationship with my wife and we have an amazing relationship now. Anil has the ability to connect with people and help them see challenges they may have and just simplify them and help us to be the real people that we are. He reminds us to not get caught up in the little things in life."

ABOUT THE AUTHOR

Anil Gupta is a gifted speaker and coach who helps people struggling with life challenges. His personal coaching and seminars on Awareness, Happiness, and Fulfillment provide individuals with the knowledge needed to transform their lives.

His seminars, personal coaching, retreats, and DVD's provide individuals with the knowledge needed to transform their lives.

Anil's extraordinary "gift" as an intuitive coach came after experiencing massive personal pains and gains himself.

Extensive training and intuitive observation help him quickly identify road blocks to better relationships, improved health and greater awareness. Awareness is the key to growth. All who have experienced Anil's gift soon discover the light within that can transform their lives.

He has a proven process that will take you through a journey leaving you empowered, fulfilled and joyous!

His passion now is to help others . . .

It is Now the right time to shine
and show us how great you are,
what your passion is and
the difference you want to make in the world.
By declaring this you will see
miracles start to happen.
The Universe is on your side.
See how you get on—if you can stand it!

PART ONE

Chapter 1

AWARENESS

If you live with awareness—you have it all!
Anil Gupta

This is the foundation stone to human existence. Yes, it sounds like a profound statement and it is. Without awareness, we would not be in existence as it is a basic tool that ensures our very existence, as well as survival.

If we were not aware of our circumstances we would have been eaten up by wild animals or poisoned by bad food. It is the awareness that lets us know what is going on in the world, what is a danger and what is not.

We, as human beings, have lost much of that innate skill as we live in safer, cleaner and abundant environments.

Your ability to master this skill will have a direct impact in the relationships and success that you have.

This one skill, if mastered, will produce abundance for you in many forms.

Suppose you wanted to fly out to New York for a short getaway. If you were to call the airline and asked the question "I want to fly to New York." What is the first question they will ask you?

- What are your travel dates?
- How many people traveling?
- How long are you staying for?
- Where are you flying from?

The most important question is—where are you flying from? You need to know where you are to get to where you want to get to. Otherwise, you will get to wherever you get to. ALWAYS.

It is vital to know where you *are* in life so that you can get to the place you *want to get to* in life.

People have targets they want to get to but if you do not know where *you are*, then how can you get to the place you are keen to get to? And how do you know whether that is truly what you are seeking?

Only through AWARENESS is this possible.

I was with my wife the other day and she said "I really want to go to a particular place."

I had the awareness or sensory acuity to see what she wanted was very important to her and what a difference it would make for her to have her wishes met. I did not always have this Awareness. That is quite an understatement actually, as for many, many years of our married life, I had no or very little Awareness. It was because of the love Meena had for me that our marriage flourished. If I can develop that skill then so can you! it is a skill that can be practiced and mastered quite easily but requires effort.

Awareness has enormous and often immediate benefits.

I remember a time when my daughter was not her usual self and I was fortunate to be aware of that. My questions about it produced no response. I had to find a way.

I was able to see that she had some sort of upset so I said "Honey, I love you very much and I know something is bothering you that is stopping you from being truly happy at this moment. I promise not to judge or chastise you for anything but lend a supporting ear to your issue. If you want to talk let's talk it over and I am sure we will find a solution."

It was entirely up to her whether she wanted help or wanted to handle the situation herself. I was not attached to her response. She received awareness of the fact that someone else noticed and became aware of the fact that it was affecting her happiness.

A quick and painless conversation followed whereby she relayed a concern that she had for a friend at school that was resolved within a few minutes.

www.ImmediateHappiness.com

Chapter 2

ACQUIRING AWARENESS

We all have the potential to become magnificent oak trees.
We are acorns that need to be in the right soil (the company we
keep), the right temperatures (our mind), the right water (growth
and contribution) and on the right path (awareness).

Anil Gupta

So how does one acquire awareness?

Step One

I recommend that you begin by watching yourself. Keep a small journal
or notepad and jot things down as they come to you. Awareness begins
when you begin to be aware of your own actions and behaviors.

Watch how your mind starts to wander and think of different things
in a matter of seconds.

Write down your thoughts that come up—there will be hundreds
of them.

Write down the judgmental thoughts that you have—I still have
them and so do you. (Yes, it is okay to admit it—we all have them!)

Write down why you do things a certain way.

Write down what you think of yourself and where that came from.

Write down what you think of others and where that came from.

Be aware of your thoughts when you think of your friends, relatives
and work mates.

As you start to become aware you will become aware of being aware and that is always interesting!

You will see yourself watching you watching you!

All of these will help you build the Awareness muscle. It will not take long before it becomes strong and producing results.

You will start to respond rather than react.

Step Two

Now you are ready for the next level. This one is fun!

Start watching other people.

In traffic, at work, while out shopping, at home—do this respectfully and not voyeuristically! It will be hard to just watch and observe but that is the ultimate goal—to become an unattached, non judgmental observer in a peaceful state.

As you progress you will find yourself being less and less judgmental and eventually you will reach a point whereby you will just observe what is going on in a passive way that leaves you untouched and unmoved by events. You will discover that you are just acknowledging things as they happen in a state of peace and with no attachment.

This is a peaceful and beautiful place whereby you will not be dragged into anything that happens in front of you. You are aware and yet detached from any outcome. Things that come to your awareness pass by like clouds in the sky.

What I have just described will give you tremendous joy and power as you realize that you can observe what happens around without having to react.

This is an advanced position to be in but it will not be long before you reach that level and you will enjoy that so much as you will just be like an observer watching a film.

You may be asking yourself "what do I get from having Awareness?" You will be in a position of tremendous power and peace that allows you to *respond* rather than *react* to any situation.

You will notice when you partner needs that extra attention, when

they feel you are not listening, when they are happy or unhappy—all of this will be effortless. Awareness works in your professional and business life.

Your response will be effortless.

Awareness is the one discipline that I value above all others—even love as you cannot fully love and be loved without it.

www.ImmediateHappiness.com

Chapter 3

YOU

If YOU empower you—
You empower your life
in many different and powerful ways.

Anil Gupta

Do you realize that you are the common denominator in whatever you do, whatever you think, wherever you go, whatever happens to you on every occasion.

So if you want your life to change *you have to change.*

It is really that simple.

So how do you change?

Firstly you have to be *aware* of who you are being, what you are thinking, what you're saying, how you are feeling, etc. You need awareness and once you have that awareness then you're able to make changes in a positive and impactful manner with almost immediate results.

In my case, I awoke one day to find that I had run my life being blissfully unaware of my arrogance, self righteousness, uncaring, egotistical, self-centeredness and I had been living by just being on autopilot.

I could not understand why I was getting the results that I was getting. I just could not work it out. Then one day after some deep soul-searching I found the answer . . . it was me!

It wasn't about the other people in my life. It wasn't about the circumstances in my life. It wasn't about the economy. It wasn't about the

government. It wasn't about where I was living. It wasn't about who I was living with. It was me.

What we have always been told is not to be egotistical or self-centered but it really has gone too far because we do need to work on ourselves.

By working on ourselves we are able to help other people. Have you ever listened to the flight attendant an airplane when they do the safety checks? What do you do when the oxygen masks come down in an emergency?

They always tell you to put the oxygen masks on yourself first, not on your children, not on your loved ones, but on yourself first.

You need to serve you first before you can serve others.

It is time to look after yourself. It is time to spend more time on you. And you are very important. I don't mean to be egotistical, self-centered or self-righteous, but just so that you know that you are important to you.

To make a difference to you first will ensure that you are performing to a very high standard. It will guarantee that you have integrity, that you have honesty and loyalty. It is to assure that you have humbleness, you have joy, you have power. It allows you to love yourself.

Here are profound yet simple truths:

If you change—your life changes.

If you change—your relationships change.

If you change—the people around you miraculously change.

If you don't believe me try for a day or so to be a different person and you'll see you will feel different—you'll be perceived differently by the people around you and they will respond differently to you.

For your life to change you have to change.

It also stems from awareness. Once you have that awareness you're no longer working on autopilot you have the ability to make changes. And even a small change can produce a big result. Here is a personal example:

My wife used to get very irritated with me because I never put the toothpaste cap back on the toothpaste tube. It really didn't

bother me but on occasions I would do it quite deliberately because it used to annoy her. No matter what she said to me, I would not listen. So one day she said something to me and my level of awareness rose considerably, she said this to me. "Honey, whenever you do not put the cap back on the toothpaste, I lose love for you."

Wow! My level of awareness made me realize that my wife did not love me as much as she could in that moment and that the simple actions I was repeating were actually causing her to lose little bits of love for me (that I immediately felt in my gut!).

What was I going to do about it? Was I going to continue not putting the lid back on the toothpaste or should I change this one simple thing—especially now that it was brought to my awareness.

What would happen if I changed?

Why should I do it?

What is the benefit to me?

These are all questions that came to my mind instantly but the overriding concept was simple—she loses love for me.

Is that what I really wanted, knowing how easy it was for me to change—literally in an instant now that I was aware of this?

Now, each and every time I look at the toothpaste tube, I always think of Meena and the great love for my wife. There is often a detectable smile on my face.

So you see, one small change produces so much more love—my capacity to love increased.

This applied to the other instances in my life which also have had significant impacts in the rest of my life because I started looking to see how I could improve my ability to be a better son, a better father, a better husband, a better friend, etc., and overall, really, a better person.

Awareness is the key.

www.ImmediateHappiness.com

Chapter 4

CAPACITY

I had often sought answers from afar when the answers were on my doorstep. You will find that you have been sitting on the treasure but have never bothered to look within to find out. Take a close look at your life—ask one question—what am I not seeing that is staring me in the face?

Anil Gupta

In the chapter on You I had informed you about the toothpaste story and how I increased my capacity to love and how I increased my capacity to be a better person.

As you become a better person, as you become aware, as you start taking action, as you start seeing results you will notice that your ability and capacity to love and be loved will increase dramatically.

Your capacity to become a better person increases, your capacity to serve others increases, your overall capacity increases. The results are immediate and quite addictive.

I remember the path that I took with my wife Meena. I remember many times I thought that I could not love her anymore than I did and that I had reached my capacity to love her. But then I grew, and my capacity to love her increased and is still increasing with even more joy. And just when I feel I have reached the capacity, it happens again and I increase my capacity again and I am filled with even more joy.

This happened with my son and my daughter and my father and my

mother and my friends. As a result, the overall person that I became was that of I having an abundance of love to give and to receive.

It is an amazing process that will bring incredible results that will have a knock on effect on other people in your life. It will make you more energized, give you a more vital life, a vibrant, joyous, blissful feeling—the sky is the limit basically.

How

How can you increase your capacity?

The fundamental way to increase your capacity is through awareness. You need to have the awareness before you can make changes. Otherwise, you are walking around in a daze or autopilot, reacting as opposed to responding.

While unaware, you are just not living a life that you want to live but rather living a life that others want you to!

Awareness is the fundamental trait I have mentioned many times, the importance of which must be repeated as it is of fundamental importance.

Awareness is the main building block of your entire life.

Awareness is the master key.

Once you have some awareness about the capacity to love, ask yourself these questions:

How can I increase my capacity

- to love
- to be loved
- to be more giving
- to be more caring
- to be kind
- to be more generous
- to live a fuller life
- to be happy
- to be fulfilled

Basically, it is the quality of questions that you ask once you have the awareness that will derive the results that you get.

It is vital to ask a quality question so that you get a quality answer. So, for example, a quality question would be "How can I be more loving in this moment?"

You have an amazing brain that is willing to serve you at all times—it will always serve you to the best of its ability.

So if you are to ask the brain the quality question it will give you quality answer. A poor quality question would've been: "Why am I not loving?" The brain will always serve you and it will give you an answer to your question. You will not like the answer!

Note the important difference in the quality and wording of the questions.

The 2nd question produced an answer which will not move you to the next level. It will not propel you to have a greater capacity. It will not endear yourself to yourself.

Quality questions will produce quality answers.

Once again, this is about awareness. Be aware of the quality of the questions that you ask yourself.

We ask ourselves questions every day, every minute of every day—these are almost like incantations and they can have a positive or negative effect depending on the quality of those incantations.

Chapter Exercise

Here is an exercise I have for you.

Get yourself a timer. For one hour, write down all the questions you may ask yourself. This is a powerful exercise where you will see how distracting your subconscious has been to your own happiness.

You need to carry on with your normal tasks and just notice and write down the thoughts that you have. For the moment, do not pay attention if they are negative or positive or if they are serving you or not serving you. This is not a time to get distracted by judgment. At this moment, just observe and write down those observations.

You will be amazed at the thoughts that you have during the day and the incantations that you have.

When you are finished, review what thoughts came and went and gain awareness to which serve your overall growth and happiness, and which do not.

Chapter 5

NAMASTE

—Clarity Brings Focus—

—Focus Brings Action—

—Action Brings Results—

—Results Brings Growth—

—Growth Brings Success—

—Success Brings Fulfillment—

—Fulfillment Brings All—

—IT IS TIME FOR CLARITY—

—Namaste—

Namaste.

That's a strange greeting, is it not?

I begin all of my seminars with this greeting. I am Indian and have used this greeting for over 50 years, but never really knew what it meant. I'll tell you what it means to me. It means "The greatness inside me honors the greatness inside you. The Divinity inside me honors the Divinity inside you. The God inside me honors the God inside you."

So imagine if you greeted everybody with those thoughts in your head. Would there be any doubt as to whether you would have a greater connection? Imagine greeting your partner in the morning by looking them in the eye (your child even) and said, "Namaste." In that moment, you are connected.

You can be fully present to each other.

Imagine if you said this to your daughter, "Honey, the greatness inside me honors the greatness inside you."

Imagine how your daughter would feel. Imagine how you would feel. This simple word could sustain you for the rest of the day.

It is incredibly powerful.

Namaste.

Chapter 6

THE JOURNEY

To lead a fulfilled and joyous life—surround yourself with people who love you for who you are and what you stand for. These people will provide you with the encouragement and true love that will nourish and inspire you. Spend less or no time with people who do not serve you—this is a vital to a truly joyous life.

Anil Gupta

We're going to take you on a journey. On this journey you'll get to a place where you'll have more love for yourself, more love for the people around you, and it's a journey that has many ups and downs, but it's a journey that you will enjoy.

On this journey I will teach you many, many tools, that you can apply in your personal, business life and professional life.

With these tools—if correctly applied—you will be able to diffuse any situation, to be in control of any situation, to be happier, to be more fulfilled. After all, that's what we're all about.

But, how do we start this journey? This journey starts from a simple notion of, "where are we?"

Remember the travel agent at the ticketing counter. You have to know where you are to be able to plan for where you are going.

Having that awareness will give you one thing that we all need, and that's clarity.

Clarity is power.

Once you have clarity, you have power.
Once you have power, you can take action.
Once you take action, you get results.
Once you get results, you get progress.
Once you get progress, it leads to success.
Success provides for happiness
And happiness leads to fulfillment.

It's really that simple, but you have to go on that journey.

You have to get the clarity first.

How Do You Get the Clarity?

Through the process and the methodologies that I'll be teaching you. How cool would it be that you got clarity? And from clarity you get all the growth, all the fulfillment that you've ever wanted.

After all, that's ultimately what we really, really want.

Clarity is Power.

Moved, Touched, and Inspired

It's incredibly powerful to get clarity. I promise you, you'll be moved, touched, and inspired. You will live with more clarity with all the riches that brings.

So how do we do this? Firstly, I would ask you to get a notebook. Just use it as you read this book. Take notes on all thoughts that come to your mind and the exercises I suggest.

At the back of the book, just write the insights that you get. And you'll get a lot of them. By doing that will allow you an easy reference place to remind yourself of all the great insights you have had.

Write Down Your Insights

And then you can always refer to the insights very quickly and reinforce them. It's very powerful. In one seminar I asked a participant, "What

was the major turning point for you?" And he said, "One sentence was the complete seminar for me."

One Sentence

There may be one thing I discuss that could resonate with you, so it's important to read through all of the book in the right order, because I do take you on a journey.

It is a process.

Start your way from the beginning and work your way to the end. Please don't go to the end and skip.

It is a proven process, it is a proven methodology, with proven results, and the results are almost instantaneous.

Have you seen my testimonials, they all say the same thing. They have received profound wisdom and profound change. The quality of their life has changed, not only has the quality of their life changed, but the quantity of their life has changed.

"Really? You mean I'm going to live longer?"

Yes, because if you're happier, you're going to be healthier. If you're healthier, you're going to live longer and you will want to live longer. And when you're surrounded by love, you're surrounded by people who enjoy you. And above all else, if you love yourself, that's the most important thing.

Loving yourself will change the feeling you have for other people. It will change the relationships they have with you; it will change the relationships that you have with them.

The most vital thing you need to do is change yourself. By you changing, your life will change, because you are the common denominator in every relationship.

YOU

I've done the research. Did you know that on the day you are born you have an average of two hundred and thirty-five relationships? Yes! It is true. The day you are born you have a midwife, you have a doctor,

you have a dentist even though you have no teeth, you have your relatives and their friends, you have your father, mother, uncles, aunts etc. The common relationship to all of these is you. You are the common denominator. For your life to change, you must change.

Please take time to work on the exercises

I'm going to give you some exercises to do. They are important to gain the maximum results. Take your time in doing them.

Be Honest

Above all else, be honest. If you're honest you can work out where you are. Honesty will bring awareness of where you are. Honesty will give you that.

Be Coachable

Be coachable, take on some of the ideas I give you. Some of them you will agree with, some of them you don't, but just take it on. By being coachable it allows you the freedom to change. Just take on what I have to say. If you don't agree with it you don't have to do it, but just try the exercises, the exercises are very important.

Trust the Process

Trust the process. It has worked, it will work, it will always work. You have to do the process in the given way.

Just 1 Sentence can make a big difference

Remember what one particular attendee said, one sentence can completely change your life. So listen out for that one sentence.

Statistic: 50%+ of Marriages Fail in Western World

We all know the statistics about marriages. Fifty percent are failing, maybe more. Although fifty percent are failing, how many people are

in a marriage that isn't serving them? How powerful would it be if you were given a tool that will allow you to pick the perfect partner? How powerful would it be if you knew what to look for? How much pain would that save you? How much pain would that save your children? A lot of pain. It will not only save you pain, it will give you pleasure. It's a win-win.

Statistics: You Would Rather Die Than Talk in Public

Do you know that people would rather die than talk in public? How crazy is that? We all love talking. What stops us from talking in public?

Fear.

And fear runs our lives. Where does the fear come from?

It normally comes from the past, something happened in the past.

Again, we're going to give you methodologies that can remove that fear. Ones that can destroy the fear. And you will get, above all else, clarity on how to do that. Clarity is, as you now know, very powerful.

I'd like you to watch a short video. This video completely changed my life. It's only three minutes long, but please, watch the video. Currently it is on YouTube at

http://www.youtube.com/watch?v=Nw0s4C0g5SM

After watching, write down how you feel. Write down the insights that you got from it. I promise you'll be moved, touched, and inspired—just by this three minute video.

For those of you with no computer access, the text follows (though it does not have the same effect as watching).

Person One: "Mrs. Lee, I believe you have some words to say about the dearly departed."

The Bereaved Widow: "I'm not going to sing praises for my late husband, not today. Neither am I going to talk about how good he was. Enough people have done that here. Instead I want to talk about

some things that will make some of you a bit uncomfortable. First off, I want to talk about what happened in bed. Ever had difficulty starting your car engine in the morning? [Snoring noises which imitate an old car not wanting to start] Well that's exactly what David's snoring sounded like. But wait, snoring wasn't everything. There was also this rear-end wind action going on as well. Some nights it would be so forceful it would wake him up. "What was that?" he would ask. "Oh, it's the dog," I would say, "go back to sleep dear." You may find this all very funny, but towards the end of his life, when his illness was at its worst, these sounds indicated to me that my David was still alive. And what I wouldn't give to hear those sounds again before I sleep. In the end, it's these small things that you remember, the little imperfections that make them perfect for you. So to my beautiful children, I hope one day, you too find yourself life partners who are as beautifully imperfect as your father was to me."

End of video

Now, write down how you felt and who you thought of while you watched this video.

　Be honest with yourself.

　Did you enjoy watching the video?

　Were you moved?

　Were you touched?

　Were you inspired?

I was.

　I'll tell you where it impacted my life.

　I used to complain about many habits of my wife, son and daughter. They would leave things lying around. They would touch my stuff. They would do things that would annoy me.

　After watching that video, when I see things on the floor, instead of complaining about it, I rejoice now. Because now I see it and I can say, "That's my son, he did that. He left that there. I love my son. I am so happy he is here."

When my wife does something that would have previously annoyed me, I now look at it in a different way. I say to myself, "My wife did that. How lucky I am." It brings me to the present that she is here, with me, and whatever it is that would have angered me is now beautifully imperfect, just as the widow discussed in the video.

I am aware and present to the fact that they are here, and I am over-flowing with gratitude for that blessing—one most of us take for granted.

You see, the circumstance hasn't changed, but how I feel about it has. So now I have chosen to be in control. I control life rather than life controlling me.

This is the start of the journey. The next steps follow now.

www.ImmediateHappiness.com

Chapter 7

HOW MUCH
DO YOU KNOW?

You need to know what you want in life. There are no lean times,
no points to reach, nowhere to get to—if you know who you are.
When you find out what you stand for and what your commitment,
purpose and mission is—you will see that time and you will
disappear. What would happen if you spent every breath
of your life doing what you know you want to do?
You would feel on top of the world!

Anil Gupta

All the Knowledge in the World

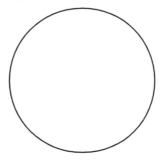

Imagine a big circle representing all the knowledge in the world.

How much knowledge do you know?

You may be surprised, but I would guess only say approximately 1%.

What You Know

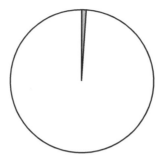

One percent is all the knowledge that you know.

What is the rest of it?

The rest is all the knowledge that you DO NOT know, right?

That's probably what I would have said too, but actually, it's not.

There's all the knowledge that we know, which is one percent.

Do you know how to fly a rocket ship?

No.

But you know that you do NOT know how to do that. Correct?

So there's what you know and there's what you know that you don't know.

What does that leave behind? Interesting, now you're thinking, aren't you? It made me think. So the balance is this, it's what you don't know that you don't know. What does that mean?

What You Don't Know

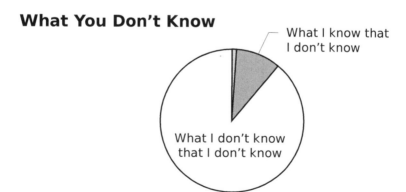

For me it means this: I'm working on my computer and I'm doing some very laborious editing. My daughter comes up to me and she says, "Dad, why are you doing it that way? Why don't you just do this and this? And you're done."

I didn't know that, but I didn't know that I didn't know that.

Does that make sense?

But that's an area that we are going to be working on and that gives you more awareness, more clarity.

My Passport

I remember a time when I had to take a flight. I was in a rush, as I always am, and I couldn't find my passport. I looked everywhere for it but I couldn't find it. What am I going to do?

Suddenly we had a blackout, I thought, "Why does this have to happen to me? I have to do something as I have a flight to catch."

I couldn't find it, my wife was out, my kids were out, I was alone in the house. I looked outside and the streetlight was on and I had a brainwave. So I went outside and started looking for my passport out there.

You may be laughing, but it was the logical thing for me to do.

A neighbor comes out and says, "Anil, what are you doing?"

I said, "Bill, I need to find my passport, will you help me?"

He said, "Sure, I'll help you," so we scrambled around looking for the passport together.

After about a few minutes, he said, "Anil, I don't see the passport here. I don't see it at all." Then he asked me a question, "Where did you drop it?"

"Well, I dropped it inside the house."

And then he looked at me and said, "You dropped it inside the house and you're looking here. Why are you looking here?"

I got a little bit irritated with him.

I thought, "What's wrong with you? I'm looking here because the light's better here. Isn't that obvious?"

It's funny, isn't it?

If you think about it logically, the light's better so it gives me a better chance of finding it.

But you know what?

That's what we do as human beings.

Imagine that you have a problem with your life in some way.

Is it not the case that we often try and find the solution in the outside world rather than the inside world. The solution is not out "there." The solutions are within.

The solutions are not hard to find.

If you focus from within then all the answers are there.

I promise you, you'll find all the answers you're looking for. The light may be better out there but that will not allow you to find what you are searching for.

Chapter 8

EXPECTATIONS

Look for the greatness in your child, nephew, niece, father, mother,
spouse, sibling, workmate, teacher, etc. There is something totally
awesome in all of us and it is quite often lost somewhere by all the
"stuff" we all have to deal with. But just stop and go within and ask
yourself this one question: "What is truly great about this person?"
You will be totally amazed at the answers you get.

Anil Gupta

We all have expectations. The problem with expectations is that they will ultimately lead to an upset. How is that? Let me explain to you. If I expect someone to be on time and they're not, I'm going to get upset. If I expect the bus to be at a particular place at a particular time and it's not or it leaves early before I get there, I'm going to get upset.

So expectations will lead to upsets.

So how do we handle that?

It's simple really. We handle that by not having expectations.

We have expectations for our friends, for our family and we have expectations for our business.

Let me ask you a question, do we have different expectations for family than we do for friends?

Yes, we do.

Our friends can do anything and we let them off, and say, "It's okay, you're my buddy, no problem" but if a family member does something

similar we have a higher expectation. We think to ourselves "Oh, they should have known, don't they know better, that's disrespectful, blah, blah, blah, blah, blah."

So by having expectations, and especially by having high expectations, you're more likely to get an upset.

By removing the expectations, the upsets will disappear.

We have different expectations for different people. I have a different one for my wife, my children, my colleagues. So being aware will allow me that freedom to not get upset.

Expectations Lead to Upsets

Expectations lead to upsets, so every time you're upset, ask yourself, "Why am I upset?"

Is it because I was expecting something to happen?

That's another tool that you've just got to use through awareness.

Whenever you get upset, ask yourself that question.

Chapter 9

FILTERS

If you were to find out that time is an illusion, that your life has made a difference and that there is nowhere to get to because you are already there—what difference would that make.

Anil Gupta

Now that you understand about expectations and that we have different expectations for different people. We also have something called filters.

We have different filters for different people.

What does that mean?

So supposing you wore orange sunglasses and you looked at a white wall, the wall would look orange. If your friend is sitting next to you and you said, "Hey, what color is that wall?" He'll say, "White."

You could have a heated argument with him if you wanted.

"No, no, no, it's orange."

"No, no, no, it's white."

"It's orange."

"It's white."

And this is what happens in a fight.

People see things in a different way.

They have different filters.

I have a different filter for my wife. I have a different filter for my son. I have a different filter for my daughter. I have a different filter for teenagers.

Some people think teenagers are loud, obnoxious, noisy. I personally think they're caring, knowledgeable, beautiful people.

It's my filter against their filter.

I have a different filter for my mother-in-law. I have a different filter for my father-in-law. I have a different filter for my hairdresser.

Can you see by using that technology of being aware that you have different filters for different people, will again give you that clarity.

Exercise:

Write down in your book, the different filters that you have. The different filters for the different people that you have and the way you listen to those people.

How do you listen to your daughter compared to your son? How do you listen to your father compared to your mother? How do you listen to your brother compared to your sister? Look at your work colleagues; you have different filter for different members of staff? Look at your friends; you have different filters for different friends?

It's important to know that you have these different filters.

It will lead to clarity.

Chapter 10

INFINITE PATIENCE

*If you want peace you have to be peaceful first, if you want love
you have to be love, if you want happiness then first be happy.
It all starts from within you.*

Anil Gupta

Infinite patience produces immediate results.

What does that mean?

What it is, is this: imagine you know you are going to get a particular result, e.g. you are going to pass a certain exam. If you know that and you have the patience to realize you have the ability to pass the exam, which is in nine days, nine weeks, or nine months, or whatever timespan, you can be calm and peaceful. You don't have to fret about it. But if you don't have that patience, you're going to fret about it, you're going to get upset and you're not going to enjoy the time leading to the exam.

My personal example is this: My son was probably about six years old and I thought he wasn't making enough progress. We Indians are high achievers and all our family members are doctors, dentists, professionals etc. etc. I thought I'd better make him step up so I brought him a tutor.

I got him some extra coaching and that went on for a number years. Then one day I realized what I was doing. I was making him wrong. I wasn't letting him grow at his own pace. I was trying to fix him and it wasn't serving me because I was tense, I was always concerned about

him and then one day I had enough, "That's it. I'm not going to do that anymore." It gave me the most tremendous relief and it allowed my son to grow. And he blossomed in a very short space of time but we also had so much more fun and peace together.

He's an incredible human being. He's got courage, energy, vitality, confidence, charisma etc. He's got everything that I have ever wanted of him and more!

Imagine how much pain I would have saved if I had infinite patience at the age of six to say, "I trust him. Everything is going to be fine, there is nothing to fix, all will be well."

It would have saved me a lot of pain. It would have saved him a lot of pain.

So infinite patience produces immediate results.

That one sentence can dramatically change the quality of your life.

Infinite patience produces immediate results.

Exercise:

Write down the areas of your life where infinite patience would benefit you. Some examples are: your child's progress, your relationships, your business progress, your progress in life, etc.

Chapter 11

WHAT YOU THINK OF ME!

Life throws us many curve balls. They are there
to make you stronger, wiser and healthier and
ultimately to a state of fulfillment.

Anil Gupta

After spending a whole day tirelessly delivering my seminar, I asked the participants what part of the seminar they enjoyed the most.

I want to share one sentence that completely altered one participant's life.

What you think of me is none of my business.

This has incredible power because it's true! We are as human beings always concerned about what other people are thinking of us—taking action upon this statement will release you from much pain.

People are going to think about whatever they are going to think about. You're not going to make any difference to them. They'll think about whatever they want to think about so let them go ahead and do it.

People are so occupied with themselves, let them be so! It's fine, it's okay. Let them think what they want.

Release their power over you. It gives you tremendous freedom and a sense of great relief.

Let's re-cap:

Clarity Brings Focus

Focus Brings Action

Action Brings Results

Results Brings Growth

Growth Brings Success

Success Brings Fulfillment

Fulfillment Brings All

www.ImmediateHappiness.com

Chapter 12

THE DATING FAÇADE

Everything that we do is for a feeling—that is it. We eat and drink for a feeling, we choose our friends and partners for a feeling that it gives us. We have cars, houses, possessions. etc., for the feeling we get. If we can control our feelings we can control our lives.

Anil Gupta

What is the dating façade?

Imagine a boy and a girl. They meet, they see each other across the room. He looks at her and says, "Wow, she's really cute. Oh, look at her hair, she's attractive. She's got a lot of friends. Oh my goodness, look at her laugh." Now he's instantly attracted to her. And she looks across the room and looks at him, "Wow, he's really cute. He's muscular, he's athletic. I like him, he's rugged, he's handsome. He's tall, he's well dressed. Just what I am looking for."

So they're attracted to each other. Then they meet, they talk and get on real well and of course one thing leads to another. Everything they both do is to please the other person.

But actually what's happening is this: she's putting on a façade. She's acting and doing things that will please him, and he is putting on a façade too because he's doing things to please her.

All of the time. Whether or not either one is conscious of this or not—they are practicing the dating façade.

Whatever she does is fantastic. "Oh my god, did you see that? She

is so amazing!" And whatever he does is perfect. "I love when he does that, he is fantastic!"

So they date and this façade goes on, and eventually they get married. And then all of a sudden he doesn't have to act to keep her happy or keep her attracted to him, so he lets down his guard and he begins to "be" himself.

And she has the same feeling and experience. "I'm married now, everything's good, I can just let go and be myself."

All of a sudden he looks at her and she looks at him and they both say the same thing: "You're not the person I married. The person I married was never like this person at all!"

And this is what happens. No one has really changed, it is just that the façade is now over because the players have become comfortable.

Imagine you could meet someone without the façade and that you could see them for who they really are. They could see you for who you really are.

How powerful would that be?

What type of relationship would you then have?

It would be authentic. There's no guard to let down, they'll see you for who you are, this is what happens in friendships. Your friends see

you as you are, warts and all. That's the definition of friendship.

You're my friend and you know more about me, you know the dirt about me, but you're still my friend. There's no façade to let down. This is why friendships work but marriages fail.

I had an arranged marriage.

I came into it with four rules. Seriously, four rules. They were:

1. Can you speak the language?
2. Are you willing to live with my parents? I'm not saying you have to, but are you willing to live with my parents?
3. You must eat meat. I didn't want a girl that didn't eat meat.
4. Do you love children and do you want children?

These were my rules. I should have asked one more: can you cook? But that's my bad. I spent the first two years of married life cooking. But she saw me as I was, I saw her as she was, that's it.

This one tip will save you so much pain, so much anguish, so much hurt.

I'm going to give you an exercise that will allow you to pick the perfect partner. It's incredibly powerful and insightful. It will save you so much pain and anguish and it will give you so much pleasure, enjoyment and vitality. If you just do this one thing.

Pick the right partner.

Pick the right friend.

Who you spend time with will determine who you become.

Exercise:

Write down your must haves for a relationship—for your perfect partner. Like a shopping list. Be honest. What are your rules? What must your ideal partner have for you to be happy?

In my live events I see people who have so many rules/ must haves that it is impossible to have any relationship that will last.

The shorter the list the greater the chance of success.

www.ImmediateHappiness.com

Chapter 13

WHAT IS LOVE?

If you want to improve your relationships,
just serve the other person with no thought about
what you will get back.

Anil Gupta

What is love? What's your definition of love? Why am I asking? Well, ultimately that's what we're all seeking, so you need to know what love is. By changing your definition of love you will change how you feel about love!

My definition of love is this: love is acceptance.

When a baby is born, to the mother it is the most beautiful baby in the world. To an observer, it's **not** the most beautiful baby in the world. The baby looks wrinkled and not beautiful at all! It is not the most beautiful thing in the world.

But what makes it so beautiful is this: the mother will accept the baby as is.

The mother will always accept the baby.

That is the greatest feeling in the world; acceptance.

Wen you accept the other person for who they are you instantly have love for that person. That definition, by itself, will make a profound difference to the way you look at people. The ability to accept will determine the quality and quantity of your happiness.

The Ability to Accept Will Determine
the Quality and Quantity of Your Happiness

Now tell me, honestly, if you use that definition of love, does that make a difference to you?

Love is acceptance.

How does your life change if your definition of love equals acceptance?

Now, with this new insight, take out your notebook again and write down areas where you can immediately apply this in your life.

What difference will it make if you immediately apply this?

What insights come to mind that you are aware of?

These notes that you're taking will make a difference to you, because it's another insight that you'll get. If you refer back to the insight you can get present to it. If you get present to it, you get awareness and that will give you a choice. The choice is then to take action or to not take action. If you do take action, you will get results immediately.

Chapter 14

BEHAVIORS

The more comfortable you are on the inside, the more comfortable you will be on the outside.

Anil Gupta

If LOVE was based purely on behavior, then perhaps none of us would have been loved as teenagers!

Seriously, if love was based purely on behavior, then let's be honest, none of us—as teenagers—would be loved.

Really, would we?

I know, I was a terrible teenager. I gave my Mum and Dad so much pain and anguish, because I was what you call a coconut.

What's a coconut? You may be asking . . .

When I was at school there were probably eight hundred white students in the school and there were three Indians. I was one of them. When I got home I was in an Indian family.

At school I'm white, at home I'm brown. Hence the coconut.

On the outside I'm brown, but on the inside I was white. I was so confused.

I didn't have any of these technologies to turn to.

I didn't know who to turn to, who to talk to. It was so confusing to me.

But now you have tools. You have these technologies that you can use.

It will make a profound difference if you put the tools I have given you to use.

And pay it forward!

You can pass these tools, technologies onto your friends, your relatives, your family, your children.

You may wish to pull out your notebook again and take a moment to write down any thoughts, ideas, insights or observations.

Chapter 15

WHO IS NUMBER ONE?

Happiness is not a pursuit. Enlightenment is not a pursuit.
It is a state. It is who you are being. It is what and how you are
experiencing. It is being present. It is a choice.

Anil Gupta

Let me ask you a question: do you make your partner number one? Or do you make your children number one?

Is your partner #1?

Are the children #1?

You must make your partner your number 1 priority to have a beautiful and fulfilling relationship.

Who do you pay more attention to?

Your children or your spouse?

I know the answer . . . ninety-nine out of a hundred times it's your children, but there's a big cost to that and I'll explain to you why.

If you make your partner number two and you make your children number one, this is what will happen: the children will realize that they are more important than your spouse.

Your spouse will feel neglected, he or she will not feel respected and he or she will lose some love for you.

So the spouse (or partner) will compensate in some manner. They'll do other things, get a hobby or they'll lose focus. That is what will happen and the children will grow up in that environment.

This will be the "model of love" you will "teach" your children without even knowing that you are teaching them.

So what will then happen when the children leave?

Spouse #1 turns to spouse #2 to give them attention, but spouse #2 already has been occupied somewhere else. They're busy, they've got their routine—they have set up their own way of being happy without the spouse.

Remember now that they've likely had that routine for fifteen or more years. And now, the children have grown up with a view to make their children more important than their spouses. And therein is the explanation of the vicious cycle.

Imagine if you could terminate that cycle right now.

You can!

Make your spouse number one.

If you make him or her number one he/she is going to feel loved and respected.

The children will see their parents making each other number one and they will do the same for their children.

They will see what a caring, loving relationship their parents had. They too will have that caring, loving relationship.

By you making your partner number one, you will create such a

strong bond, such a great feeling amongst yourselves that it will give you great joy and great pleasure.

Remember that your own children will see this and their kids will feel that sense of love. You must realize that you are not neglecting your kids, but rather, you are empowering them. You are giving them the vitality, the energy, the tools, so that they too can have a relationship like yours. Your capacity to love increases—your children receive even more love!

My wife is totally number one.

She's my goddess.

The children come number two.

She's my number one priority. I look after her as my number one priority. She looks after me as her number one priority. My kids see that, they will do the same. If you meet my kids you will see happy, beautiful, joyous, grounded, centered and loving kids.

You have to make your partner number one.

It will save your relationship!

Exercise:

Write down the ways you can make your partner #1.

Some examples of this are:

- Serve his or her needs first
- Talk to them more
- Give them attention
- Pamper them
- Make them feel special
- Spend time alone
- Have outings together
- Hold hands
- Have a "date night"
- Play more
- Go out for an ice cream
- Praise, love and respect them.
- Take notice of a new hair style, outfit, etc.

www.ImmediateHappiness.com

Chapter 16

MEANING-MAKING MACHINES

If you mainly focus and become stronger on the inside then you will become stronger on the outside too—work from the inside out for a fulfilled life.

Anil Gupta

As human beings, we make everything mean something.

Everything.

Something happens, we make it mean something. For me, if you don't return my call it means you don't love me, care for me, or respect me!

What actually happened was—you did not return my call.

We are meaning-making machines.

Have a look at your life.

What do you make things mean?

Oh, my wife didn't do this, it means that she doesn't love me. Or my wife did this, she should have done that, that means she doesn't respect me etc., etc.

Once you think about it, you will realize this happens on automatic pilot. We instantly make these decisions.

Where in your life do you make things mean something?

If you begin to be conscious and aware of it you will find yourself remembering, when your son says something you make it mean something. "Oh, he's being disrespectful, he's not listening, I've told him

many times, why doesn't he listen?"

Sound familiar?

What we need to do is this: we need to separate what we make something mean and what actually happened. So, for example, if someone doesn't call me back, I make it mean they don't care, they don't respect me, etc. But what actually happened was this: they did not call me back.

That's all that happened. End of story.

Stop attaching YOUR meaning to THE circumstance and you will save yourself so much pain, worry, and grief.

Exercise:

Please write down the following:
- What do you make things mean?
- What actually happened?
- How does this impact your life?
- What would happen if you gave it a different or no meaning?

How many times do we make things mean something? Be honest. The answer is: every single time.

"Oh, my wife gave me the look. The look means she's upset." All that happened was this: my wife looked at me in a particular way, that's it. It doesn't mean anything. We're always looking for meaning. When you look for a meaning you'll always find it. Because as human beings we love to be right.

Chapter 17

BEING RIGHT

*It is the journey not the destination that gives joy to your lives!
You will find that the obstacles you had faced had been created by
you. Once you get this awareness you are on the journey to joy.*

Anil Gupta

Humans love to be right.

It's true.

I know that. You know that. We all know that!

We have fights. After a while, in that fight, you think, "What am I fighting about?" Because you've forgotten. But you want to be right so you continue the fight just to be right about it and then you'll be right about being right.

Am I right?

Yeah, I'm right, I know I'm right!

If you know that humans are meaning-making machines, if you know that humans love to be right, you can do something about it, you can take action.

You can stop the vicious cycle and you can stop it in an instant.

Exercise:

Please write down the following:

- Where have you been right?
- With your partner?

- Children?
- Work mates?
- Family?
- Friends?

Chapter 18

THE SPEEDBOAT

Have you ever been in a boat? Yes, of course you have. So imagine this: the boat's going along and behind you there is the wake, which is all the turbulence.

So let me ask you a question: what propels the boat forward?

Is it the engine or is it the wake (the turbulence behind the boat)?

Think about it. If you took the boat and put it into a still pond, there's no turbulence there, so if it goes forward it would be the engine, correct?

So the engine propels the boat forward, correct?

I think we can all agree on that.

Let me give you a representation: the engine is you, the engine is me. We are the propeller, the engine, everything. We are the boat. The future is where the boat is going to go and the past is where the boat has been.

So what propels us into the future?

For a lot of us it's the past, it's the wake.

The past determines our future, but that's not the case in reality.

We determine the future we want to live into.

Not the past, but a lot of us live a life where the past equals the future.

So imagine that you are driving a car and you are looking at the rearview mirror. What's going to happen? Yes, you're going to crash. That's what's going to happen to you if you keep on living in the past. You're going to crash.

You're going to get the same results and if you keep on getting the same results then that's the definition of madness, it's insanity. I know, I've been there, I've done it many times, but I was on auto-pilot. It was incredibly painful for me. I got a huge insight—a painful insight, but I got it. As soon as I got it I took action. Immediate results will follow.

Exercise:

Write down where in your life the past has been creating your future.

- Past relationships
- My past friendships
- My past relationship with my parents
- My childhood
- My bad experiences, etc.

Chapter 19

QUALITY OF QUESTIONS

The results you are getting is due to who you are being and to
change the results all you have to do is change who you are being.
Are you being a victim? Are you energized? Are you loving?
Are you a great parent, child, sibling? Are you taking action?
Are you knowledgeable in your field? etc.
What questions can you ask yourself to be better?

Anil Gupta

The quality of your life is totally dependent upon the quality of the questions you ask yourself.

I have to thank Tony Robbins for that profound life lesson. It is true. The quality of your life is dependent on the quality of the questions you ask yourself.

I used to ask very stupid questions myself "Why are you so stupid? Why did you do that? Why did you do that, again! Are you crazy ? Does she love me ? Why does this keep happening ?"

All of these things used to go through my mind and I would get appropriate responses back from my brain. That is the way the brain works! I know there is similar dialogue in your head too.

Why do you keep doing that?

You know that if you ask a silly question, you'll get a silly answer.

So you need to ask more empowering questions and hence you will receive more empowering answers.

59

So the more empowering question becomes "how could I change the questions I ask myself?"

I could say, "Hey, what am I learning from this? How could I change this? What can I do differently? What am I learning?"

How, what, when—a number of better quality questions.

Once you ask a quality question you will get a quality answer.

Exercise:

Write down what kind of questions you ask yourself.

- Why do I do this?
- Why do I get the same results?

Whatever the questions you ask, write it down then ask a better question to replace it with.

- How can I do a better job here?
- How can I learn from this?
- How can I serve my wife better?
- How can I serve my child in a better way?

By asking quality questions like that you'll get better answers. It's that simple. But please write these things down, because from here you get that awareness.

For your life to change, you have to change.

It's simple.

Chapter 20

THE COMMON DENOMINATOR

No matter what you do it is impossible to change the past. But, starting from this very moment onwards you have the ability and duty of being able to create your new ending that will serve you and others. The truth cannot be challenged. What is your new ending? It is time to start it!

Anil Gupta

Do you realize that you are the common denominator in every relationship and everything that you do, think, feel or say. All of your relationships have one thing in common—YOU.

By you changing, it is a fact that everything around that common denominator (YOU) changes instantly—in other words, everything around you changes.

So you have to change and it's how you change, when you change, what you change that will make the difference.

- How you change
- When you change
- What you change

This book serves as a guide to a process. To get the best results, you must follow the process.

Write down your insights AND write down the actions you're going to take. Keep the journal or notebook handy and refer back to it frequently.

www.ImmediateHappiness.com

Chapter 21

COMMUNICATION

It is not what happens in life but who you become. Do obstacles stop you or fire you up? How great can you be? Ordinary people can do extraordinary things. How? Through everything being in alignment, full awareness and being in the now.

Anil Gupta

Your relationship will thrive when you have great communication. Your communication with yourself is the first step to take. Improve the quality of the communication you have with yourself and your communication with the outside world will change—immediately.

Be comfortable in your own skin, be happy, be strong.

Talk to yourself in a positive way.

Have the power within.

How do you communicate with people?

- Do you communicate enough?
- Do you communicate too much?
- Is the quality of the communication good enough?

Remember,

It's _Not_ the Quantity; It's the Quality

Relationships fail because of lack of communication.

As an example, let me share this scenario with you on an everyday occurrence with a partner.

Option one: I say to my wife: "I love you."

Option two: I say to my wife: "Honey, I love the way you treat me. I love the way you care for me. I love the way you look. I love the way you look after our children. Honey, you make my life so much more joyous and beautiful. Thank you so much for being in my life."

Do you see the difference in how you can communicate?

- What do you say?
- HOW do you say it?

The difference, in my relationship with my wife, when I made this communication adjustment has been profound. And yet the action itself took all of a few seconds.

A few seconds to save your marriage!

When I speak like this to my wife, she is positively energized for hours. She'll do anything for me, and vice versa. I'd do anything for her.

Exercise:

- How can you adjust or tweak your communication to make it more effective?

Chapter 22

LISTENING

*There is a reason why your relationship is not as good as it was—
you have stopped making that person important and loved the
way you used to. All you have to do is serve them. If they are your
partner then make them your # 1 priority—above anything else. The
relationship will improve and blossom. Yes, it really is that simple.*

Anil Gupta

Listening is Communication

We have two ears for a reason—so we can listen more than we speak.
Your ability to listen will greatly increase the quality of any relationship in your personal, business or family life. Listening attentively will
allow you to get all the facts and the speaker will feel listened to—that
makes a such a difference. You will receive immediate benefits. Eye
contact is communication. I can look at my wife. Four seconds, that's
all it takes. We're connected, we have this non-verbal communication
that says a thousand words of love and respect. Four seconds. Imagine
that in your life.

Your relationships will thrive, you will thrive. You will have more
energy, more vitality, more power, more enjoyment—all just by adjust-
ing your communication.

It is a skill that you need to practice, practice, and practice. The
rewards are enormous.

Exercise:

- Where can you communicate better?
- Who can you communicate better with?
- How would that impact your life?
- What is stopping you taking action?

Chapter 23

GRATITUDE

*Look for the beauty no matter what! You are surrounded by
many beautiful and amazing things that you take for granted.
Have a close look at your hands—a really close look. Do you
see their beauty, how they have served you for so many years.
What would you do without them? Have a look around you
and your awareness will be upgraded!*

Anil Gupta

Gratitude is vital.

Why is it vital?

Because it is the secret to success and fulfillment.

You cannot be successful without having gratitude.

Let me share something that happened to me. I was in India and
had to get up early to catch a flight. I was waiting at the taxi rank to
get a ride to the airport and I happened to look across the street and
saw some people sleeping in the street. One of the men got up with a
big smile on his face. He went to the water pump and just threw water
on his face and he had an even bigger smile on his face. Ah, the simple
pleasure of cool water on one's face. He was so present to it and so
grateful for it.

I witnessed that and I realized that I was so upset.

I asked myself, "Why are you upset?"

My answer came suddenly from within: "I'll tell you why I am upset.

Because that guy is sleeping in the street. He has nothing but I have much more and yet in this moment, he is much happier than me."

It annoyed me and it upset me, but I asked myself one quality question: "Why is he so happy and you're not?"

As I went through the day, the question dominated my thoughts. I could not find the "right" answers and then, as suddenly as the original insight came, I found my answer, again from within.

Because he made a choice, he was grateful for what he had. He had no expectations.

I realized that I was not grateful at all.

I had chosen to be living in my head instead of in the present moment and in gratitude and without expectation.

My inner dialogue sounded something like this: "I'll be happy when 'this' happens. I'll be happy when 'that' happens."

I had to get up early. I was focusing on the wrong things. I was not being grateful for what I have. I was expecting something to happen and it didn't happen. I could not get rid of everything that was "wrong" with my thinking.

He was grateful and he had no expectations for the day.

He may not have been fed that day, but he had something that I could never have in that moment, and that was gratitude, and a sense of fulfillment.

A powerful lesson.

So no matter where you are in life if you have gratitude, you have success.

Exercise:

What can you be grateful for?

Write down fifty things you can be grateful for. I know what you're thinking, "I can't write fifty things down."

Yes you can and you must.

If your mind is drawing a blank, then start off with this: start off with something simple.

- Be grateful that you have a hair (anywhere!).
- Be grateful that you have a nose.
- Be grateful that you have an eye. Two? You are lucky!
- Be grateful that you have arms and legs.
- Be grateful that you have your health.
- Be grateful for the smallest things in life.
- Be grateful that you're alive.
- Be grateful that you can breathe.

Now grow the list. This is a muscle you need to exercise.

Write down one hundred things you can be grateful for.

This exercise will be transformational for you, because it will change your focus and make you present in the moment.

Dig deep and really pull out all of the blessings you have to be grateful for.

If you change your focus you change your life.

Okay, you've done that exercise.

How many things did you write down?

Did it make a difference?

I know it did.

The more grateful you are, the happier you are.

Please, wherever you go, whatever you do, live in a state of gratitude. This will become a habit and you will get better and better at it. It truly is a road to happiness.

This exercise has a second part.

Who can you be grateful to?

Write down all the people you can be grateful to.

- your mother
- your father
- your brother
- your husband
- your wife
- your business associate
- your friend at school
- the teacher that spent the extra time with you
- the mentor who guided you and coached you and nurtured you to better things
- the person who stood up for you
- the random stranger who helped you

Write down their names.

Write down what they did for you.

And the next step is to go and THANK THEM.

In this section, I would like to acknowledge and thank my wife. Meena Gupta.

She's an incredible human being.

She has stood by me.

She has coached, guided and nurtured me.

Even though at times I didn't deserve it she stood by me all of the time.

She gave me the greatest strength, and continues to do so.

She stood by me when things weren't going right, when things were going really bad.

I remember a time, she said, "Honey, I don't care if we lose everything as long as I'm with you."

Imagine how I felt when she said that. Filled with love and hope.

When she said that I knew that I had nothing to worry about.

I relive such moments to keep my awareness and gratitude at high levels.

Take the few extra moments to thank the people in your life.

It will make a difference to you, it will make a difference to them.

In fact, you have a duty to thank them.

www.ImmediateHappiness.com

Chapter 24

THOUGHTS

I just coached a man who thought he had no wealth. I asked him to write down 50 things to be grateful for. He realized he was wealthy! My definition of wealth is this: wealth is what you have left after all your possessions are taken away from you.

Anil Gupta

You experience life through your thoughts.

So what do you think about every day? Your relationships will change if you change your thoughts. How do you think about your wife or about your children? Are they positive or are they negative?

When I think of my son or daughter I often place my hand over my heart and tears well up in my eyes—happy tears of joy.

I instantly feel incredibly positive and joyous that they have brought so much joy to our lives.

My wife. Oh my goodness. She's incredible. You know when I think of her I think of joy and love and of peace. I think of commitment, the love that she has for me. The dedication she has for me. All positive nurturing thoughts.

My dad is an incredible, incredible man. He is the reason I'm here. Without him I wouldn't be here. I have the greatest love for my dad. He touches, moves and inspires so many people. Very humble. He doesn't want anything. His needs are simple. You should meet my dad.

How do you think about your loved ones? Do you see their beautiful

uniqueness and gifts? Or do you have negative thoughts?

Remember, your thoughts will determine your relationships.

Change your thoughts and your relationships will change.

Upsets

If you have an upset in a relationship, by changing the thoughts you have in that relationship will change that relationship. It's that simple and it's that fast.

You are what you think about.

You carry every relationship in your head.

Present Now

My mother was an incredible woman, but I never knew how incredible she was until after she died. People told me what she did for them, how she impacted their lives. What a difference she made.

Sadly, I didn't know that until after the fact.

I wished I'd have asked her.

I wished I had spent more time with her.

I wished I had the courage to ask her these questions, but I didn't know.

Please, don't make the mistake I made, communicate with your father. Communicate with your mother. Ask them questions on how they were brought up. Ask them questions about their lives. Spend time with them.

I made a biography for my dad.

I video recorded him so I could see his face forever. His face lights up when he talks about the past. When he starts talking about one subject, he'd remember something else and you'd see his face change. I recorded that, for myself and for my children so that we could carry the essence of that connection, that love, that history.

This is what communication is.

You need to know what is going on in other people's lives. It's important, it's vital. It's not difficult to do that. Just ask simple questions.

"Hey dad, what was it like growing up? Dad, what did you use to do when you were a kid? Really? I didn't know that about you."

Watch his face.

Watch your mum's face when you ask questions like that.

They'll light up, because no matter what happens, your parents are totally responsible for you being on this planet, without them you wouldn't be here, so you have to have gratitude for your parents.

By having gratitude for your parents will make a difference to your life immediately.

www.ImmediateHappiness.com

Chapter 25

PAIN AND SUFFERING

Adversity is your friend—embrace it and stop fighting it. The calmness will produce a new you that you may have never seen but it will propel you to greatness and give you clarity. Adversity is not to be feared but look at it with gratitude and your life will change. It may not be easy but it will make you grow and thrive.

Anil Gupta

Are you in pain or are you suffering?

What's the difference?

Well pain is this: pain is when things are not going the way you want them to go or things should not be a certain way—this is both physical and mental.

If the economy is not going the way it is supposed to be going. If your job is not going the way you want it to be going. If your relationship isn't going the way you want it to be going, that's painful.

If that is pain, what is suffering?

Suffering is when you feel hopeless, helpless, or powerless or when there's no hope.

So imagine that you have a relationship and you don't feel there's any hope. There is going to be suffering for you. A relationship that is not working or going the way you want it to go is going to be painful.

How do you remove the pain?

How do you remove the suffering?

Good question to which the answer is "You do it by changing you."

Much like the quality of questions you will be asking—it starts from within YOU. It begins by changing your thoughts, by changing your actions, by changing your visions, by changing your expectation, by changing YOU.

By changing any of these things, you will create a small shift that will create another shift that will create another shift. Much like a domino effect.

So you have to change your thoughts, your actions, your feelings, and that will change your relationship to pain and suffering.

Exercise:

- What has been making you feel pain?
- What has been making you suffer?
- How can you resolve or shift these feelings to a powerful resolution?
- What expectations do you have?
- How aware are you?
- Have you taken action? Is more action necessary?

Chapter 26

LETTING GO

Resentment is allowing someone to have power over your life without a remote control.

Anil Gupta

What are you holding onto in your relationship, in your business, in your personal life, in your family life?

What are you holding onto? Why are you holding onto it?

Write it down. If you are holding it, it must have importance to you.

I have no idea what you just wrote but I can tell you this. I can tell you why you are holding onto it. It is because you want to be right.

As human beings we love to be right. We discussed this earlier, remember. This is just another place in your life where it creeps in to bring you unhappiness.

"Oh, she did this to me. Oh, he did that to me."

We love to be right, but remember, there's a huge cost to being right.

We lose connection.

We lose love.

We lose vitality.

We lose energy.

We lose self-expression.

And there's a reason we don't want to let go, because if we let go, then they win.

But there's no winning here.

The only person that loses is you.

Because it affects everything that you do.

Letting go will release you from the pain and constraints of the past—IMMEDIATELY.

It takes strength, courage, and will power to let go, but the rewards are so worth it.

I remember I had some business partners many, many years ago who cheated me. I wouldn't let go and it was burning me up inside. It was making me sick.

As soon as I was able to let go I got my freedom back, I got my energy, my vitality, my happiness back.

So what is it you're not letting go of?

Why are you not letting go of it?

What is the emotional and financial cost of holding on?

You've already been given many tools, use some of the tools you've been given.

Exercise:

Write down the following:

- All the things you are holding onto
- How does this impact your life?
- Why won't you let go?
- What are the benefits of letting go?

Resentments

We also have resentments in life.

And resentments cost us dearly.

Resentments are like this Chinese proverb: If you have revenge in mind, you'd better dig two graves.

Resentment is like being bitten by a snake twenty years ago and the venom is still inside your body. But the venom is imaginary, we made it up, but we can feel it, taste it, hear it, see it. It's imaginary, but we make it so real.

How ridiculous is that?

If you're bitten twenty years ago by a snake, why would you still hold onto it?

Because we love to be right.

But being right always costs us.

What is a quick way to let go of the need to be right?

To be able to forgive.

To be able to forgive will give that freedom back to us.

To get that freedom back will completely change the quality of your life.

The express pathway to freedom is through forgiveness.

This is incredibly important.

All the tools I've been giving you have led us to this position, because we need to forgive.

www.ImmediateHappiness.com

Chapter 27

YOU ARE IN CHARGE

*It is our choice. We can choose to be
happy and fulfilled.*

Anil Gupta

When you forgive you realize that you have been in charge all along. You have chosen to be unhappy and now you can choose to be happy.

Now, you can choose to feel freer because you know that the past is not the future.

You're in charge, you have the power.

What to do now? How cool would it be if you became the director, the producer, the casting director, the cameraman—everything, in your own movie.

You get to be the main actor, you get to direct. You get to decide what you do, how you do it, when you do it, everything. You are in charge of your own movie.

Once you are able to let go and forgive, you discover that you don't have other people running your movie anymore. You're it, you're the hero. You become the main actor, you decide how you want to do things from now on. How cool is that?

You write the script. You produce it, direct it, everything.

How fun would that be?

Exercise:

Allow your fantasies to run free in this one. If you were writing the perfect movie of your life, what would it look like?

What kind of a character are you? Who is your partner?

Who are your friends? What do you do?

Are you happy or a drama queen?

Is your movie an action flick or a romance?

Is it a "feel good" movie with a happy ending?

Remember—it's YOUR movie.

Chapter 28

MUSTS AND SHOULDS

Acceptance is the key to happiness.

Anil Gupta

Remember, I had four musts when I got married. Once again, mine were:

1. Speak native language
2. Be willing to live with my parents
3. Non-vegetarian
4. Must love kids

Now you need to realize that the more musts you have for your partner, the more problems you'll have. The more musts you have for your business or family—the more problems you will have.

I've had participants who have stated their musts at events.

They produce a huge list of what their partner must have and the realize that their list is far too long! How realistic are such expectations?

So the simple formula would look like this:

Less "Musts" + Easier "Musts" =
Successful Relationships

So, what is a good example of realistic musts?

"They must be honest."

"They must be caring/loving."

"They must love children"

"They have to be faithful."

Think of it this way—a must is really non-negotiable. It is something that you value greatly in your life and you are not flexible with. Honesty and fidelity are usually a must.

What's a should?

A should is something you like, but not necessarily a must.

A must for one person may be a should for another and vice versa.

Here are some sample lists from things that my past event participants listed.

Possible Musts

Handsome, Tall, Nice Car, Loves Children, Athletic, Faithful, Honest, Single, Financially Secure, Not Been Married, Passionate, Respectful, Athletic, Adventurous, Intimate, Caring, Playful, Funny, Romantic, Non-Smoker, Social Drinker, Loves Animals.

Possible Shoulds

Likes Animals, Likes Children, Nice Massages, Playful, Adventurous, Athletic, Financially Secure, Professional, Never Been Married, Tall, Older Than Me, Patient, Respectful, Punctual, Handsome, Gentlemanly

Now remember these are merely suggestions—the way you prioritize depends upon your values and beliefs.

Exercise:

Write down what is important to you!

Then honestly review your answers.

What are your musts and shoulds?

Communication is vital here—ask your partner what is a must and what is a should—you will be very surprised! Once you know what their musts and shoulds are you can then make sure they are all provided.

- What can I do for you?
- How can I do it?

By asking a better quality question, which is what we're doing, you'll get a better quality answer.

By communicating you're getting results.

By communicating you're getting honest feedback and you can take action. You can focus on the exact must or should you need to focus on. So again, we're using all the tools here.

Meaning-Making Machines

What meaning is your partner putting to this? The likely meaning they are putting to this is "Wow, my partner really cares for me."

Where Can You Use It?

You can use it for your family, business and personal life.

Exercise:

Go over your musts and shoulds list. Can anything be moved over from musts to shoulds and does something have to be moved from shoulds to musts ?

Think about cach trait you wrote down.

Is a must really a must or is it a should?

By changing a must to a should can open up something for you, it will allow you to have a wider choice, more flexibility in any situation or relationship.

Changing a "must" to a "should" will bring more clarity in your relationships.

Your list and awareness of your musts and shoulds is incredibly powerful and insightful.

Let me share another way you can use these tools:

Supposing you're looking for an employee. Write down what your musts are, write down what your shoulds are. Make sure that your musts are satisfied. As a business owner the most important thing you can do is pick the right person to work for you. This technique will save you much pain.

Chapter 29

WHO YOU SPEND TIME WITH

The making, keeping and nurturing of friends is both a science and an art. It is important to learn these skills—if you have friends you have the world.

Anil Gupta

Who you spend time with is who you will become. So in a similar way we separated the musts and shoulds in the previous chapters, now we will rate the quality of our relationships based on how we feel within the relationship.

I'm going to give you this great exercise now. I would like you to write down all of the people that you spend time with during the week.

Write their names down.

Against their names write down how many hours a week you spend time with them.

I would like you to do one more thing.

Against the name, write down their grade—A, B, or C.

An "A" friend is someone who is positive and encourages you, inspires you, moves, touches, and really cares for you. They are really up there and always support you.

A "B" friend is someone who are good people, you enjoy their company, they're okay. The do not pull you down or inspire you.

A "C" friend is someone who sucks the energy out of you, takes time

off you. You don't really feel energized and if you were honest with yourself, you'd agree that they waste your time. They are generally a huge negative in your life.

Exercise:
- Write down your friend's name.
- Write down how many hours a week you spend with them.
- Grade them A, B, or C.

Now look at your list. Have a look at the names you've written down. Have a look at how many A's, how many B's and how many C's you have.

Look at the time you spend with "A", "B" or "C" people.

Who you are is dependent on who you spend time with.

It's real simple and should be obvious to analyze the results. If your time is filled with negative and energy sucking "C" people then you know why your life feels as it does.

"Why are you spending so much time with a C?"

After doing this exercise, they instantly get it. They know why they're not succeeding.

So, look at how much time you spend with a C, look how much time you spend with an A. Spend more time with the A's. Spend less time with the C's or even better, no time.

Why are you spending time with C's?

Are you enabling C's?

Are you encouraging them?

By cutting off the C's you're empowering them, you're doing them a favor, because they'll get it. By spending more time with them you are enabling them. Makes sense?

If there are members of your family putting you down, I say don't spend time with them.

You don't have to. Not if it's pulling you down.

I've made that shift in my life. It's incredibly powerful and it's incredibly freeing. I don't spend time with people who pull me down,

I don't care who they are. I just don't do it.

It's not empowering them, it's not empowering me.

Where else can you apply this?

- Business
- Personal
- Family
- Spouse/Partner

www.ImmediateHappiness.com

Chapter 30

CEASE FIRE

Do you ever have fights?

How would you like a technique to stop any future fight dead in its tracks!

My wife and I had a ton of fights at one time. A ton of fights that would get out of hand. We wouldn't talk for days. And one day I thought, "I don't want this anymore." I asked myself a better question, "How can I stop this?"

But I love to be right and I love to be right about being right, so it took me a while to get the answer. Then one day I got the answer. This is how we stopped fights and if you use this tool you will never, ever, ever have a fight again. I promise you.

It works like this:

My wife and I sat down and said, "Honey, I don't want to have a fight with you anymore." She says, "I know, I don't want to fight with you. Why do we fight?"

We fight because of disagreements.

You're being right, I am being right. You want to hold onto your position, I want to hold onto my position.

So what if we make an agreement that whenever we use one word that we both agree on, if either of us use that word, under any circumstance, no matter how bad or how right we are, we have to stop fighting.

So we agreed a mutually significant word that had meaning for us.

The word we use is *ceasefire*. It means something to us.

It does work and I tell you it is annoying when first used!

When we start having a fight and it's getting out of hand, we just want to stop whatever it is we're going through, one of us will say the word "ceasefire" and we've got to stop, because we made that agreement.

There were times I didn't want to stop. But after only a few uses of that word the fighting stopped as we knew it was futile to carry on anyway—it was like a nuclear deterrent!

I have had to use it on her; she has had to use it on me.

It works every single time.

So pick a word that works for you.

I've had the following words from different people at different events: "Las Vegas," "Napoleon," "chocolate," all sorts of words that can work for them, that can work for you.

Just do that and it's very, very powerful.

No more fights, nothing getting out of hand.

This is another very simple and yet instantly powerful technique, this simple exercise will make a difference to you.

Chapter 31

MAGICAL MOMENTS

We all have a duty to share our
knowledge, love, and gifts.

Anil Gupta

Have you ever had a moment that you would classify as magical? Sure you have!

Write down experiences you have had with your spouse, children, parents and with your friends. If you allow yourself to remember and reminisce, you will realize that there are hundreds of them.

My family always writes down our MMs when we go on vacation in our Magical Moments book.

Whenever you feel down, upset, or don't feel so great, look at that book.

Read a sentence, because what you focus on is what you get.

If you focus on the day your son is born, I guarantee you, you will have a happy thought even when he is now in front of you as a teenager who just got into trouble.

Choose to focus on something positive, and if you put everything down in that magic moments book you can stack up great moments and great feelings that can also be a part of your toolkit for success and happiness.

We have read our MM's many times over—if we had not written them down we would have forgotten so many of them.

You can go back to that time to get that same feeling back.

www.ImmediateHappiness.com

Chapter 32

ONE PHONE CALL

You must work on yourself to reach fulfillment; emotionally,
spiritually, mentally and physically.

Anil Gupta

If you had one hour to live who would you call?

It's a profound question if you think about it and really allow yourself to "play" as though it is true.

What feelings come up for you?

My next question should be obvious if you have read this far and done the exercises in the book. Why are you waiting?

Write down who you would call and then, gather the strength and the courage to please call them.

- Tell them what they mean to you.
- Tell them how much you love them.
- Tell them how much you care.
- Tell them what you think about them.

Don't wait.

There's a time for urgency for the people that you care about.

That time of urgency is now.

Put the book down.

Go do it.

Tell them.

"Dad, I thank you for everything you've done for me. I thank you for looking after me. Thank you for coaching me, guiding me. Thank you for putting up with me when I wasn't being the nicest of people, when I was being quite stupid, really. But thank you for seeing the greatness inside of me. Thank you for being so forgiving. Dad, I'm so grateful to you. I love you so much. Thank you."

How long does that take?

Less than a minute.

I guarantee you, if my son said that to me I would be inflated, I would be over the moon. I know you would too. The things we can do to change other people's lives will change our lives and it will change our children's lives.

So let's do it.

Exercise:

Call that someone special now and tell them how you feel about them and thank them.

Chapter 33

DAILY CLEARANCES

Working on you will produce the best results you will
ever get—you will become fulfilled.

Anil Gupta

We all have things that go on during the day.

Here is another great exercise to do with your family. You can even do it with your staff or with your family.

The exercise is: sit the family around a table and have a daily clearance.

So for example, in our family we would sit around a table and I would ask people, (around the table; my wife, my son, my daughter) "is there anything that you have on your mind, any upset that hasn't been resolved?"

Someone will come up and say, "I was not acknowledged for doing this or that." I respond, "Wow, I didn't even know that." But it was on their minds, so then what we do is we acknowledge them and work to have that issue resolved.

This daily clearance creates tremendous trust and communication as well as awareness in the family ensuring that no resentments or issues are left unresolved.

How powerful would that be as a family?

- How powerful would that be in a business?
- How powerful would that be with your friends?

This is a simple exercise. When we do it as a family it's the smallest things that come up. We take it in turns to run the "meeting." This empowered our children tremendously.

I remember a time, I think my daughter was seven, she led the meeting. She was the one whose turn it was to ask, "Has anyone not been acknowledged for anything, has anyone got any incompletions?"

Can you imagine the power that she had at the age of seven? Imagine your children, your nieces, your nephews, having that power.

Just through a simple technique.

Chapter 34

TWO MAGIC WANDS

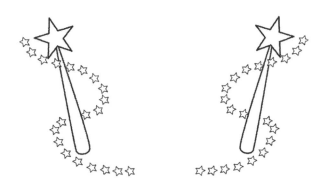

If you were given two magic wands—one to have all the money in the world and the second was for all the happiness in the world—what would you chose?

A lot of people would choose all the money in the world because that would bring them happiness, but is that really the case?

The people who take all the money in the world are looking for a feeling. The feeling that they're looking for is a sense of security. The sense from having that money. So they don't actually want the money, they just want the feeling from having that money.

If you could generate that feeling, that will give you fulfillment, power, joy and happiness.

So we're all after one thing: a feeling, a feeling of gratitude, a feeling of love, a feeling of fulfillment. That's all that we're after, a feeling.

Everything that we do, we do for a feeling.

www.ImmediateHappiness.com

Chapter 35

GREATNESS

Whenever you meet someone, see the greatness inside them, see the goodness inside them.

Acknowledge them.

- "Hey, you have great hair."
- "Wow, I love your eyes."
- "Thank you for serving us. I've never had such great service."
- "Thank you. I really appreciate that, that was very kind of you."

Once you start seeing the greatness in other people it becomes a habit and you'll see more greatness. Once you acknowledge other people they'll do anything for you. It's a feeling that we all want, to be useful, to be of service, to be appreciated.

"I have been using these tools in my life and the results are phenomenal. I feel powerful, strong, balanced, loved, and loving, with a purpose to my life. I recommend these tools to all age groups. The sooner you start, the better the results. Give this gift to the people you love, you'll make a difference in their lives."

Anu Gupta

Namaste

Greatness inside me honors the greatness inside you.
The divinity inside me honors the divinity inside you.
The love inside me honors the love inside you.

I made you a promise that you would be moved, touched, and inspired, and I'm certain that if you followed our exercises, if you followed our coaching, that you will be greatly moved, touched, and inspired.

If you have people in your life that you love, the greatest gift you can give them is a copy of this book, attend a live event, use the DVD series. They will thank you for the rest of your life. This technology works at any age group. It will release you from the constraints of the past.

You get to master your life instead of life mastering you. With the greatest amount of love and humility—I say, to you:

Namaste.

Chapter 36

USE WHAT YOU NOW KNOW

Before we proceed to the final and most powerful chapter on forgiveness, it is essential to just review the tools that you have been given.

NAMASTE	QUALITY OF QUESTIONS
AWARENESS	THE COMMON DENOMINATOR
YOU	COMMUNICATION
CAPACITY	LISTENING
THE JOURNEY	GRATITUDE
HOW MUCH DO YOU KNOW	THOUGHTS
EXPECTATIONS	PAIN AND SUFFERING
FILTERS	LETTING GO
INFINITE PATIENCE	YOU ARE IN CHARGE
WHAT YOU THINK OF ME!	MUSTS AND SHOULDS
THE DATING FAÇADE	WHO YOU SPEND TIME WITH
WHAT IS LOVE?	CEASE FIRE
BEHAVIORS	MAGICAL MOMENTS
WHO IS NUMBER ONE	ONE PHONE CALL
MEANING-MAKING MACHINES	DAILY CLEARANCES
BEING RIGHT	TWO MAGIC WANDS
THE SPEEDBOAT	

Please review your notes and the book before going to the next chapter.

www.ImmediateHappiness.com

Chapter 37

FORGIVENESS

The quality of your life is determined by the quality
of the forgiveness that you are able to give,
both for others and for yourself.

Anil Gupta

Please make sure you have reviewed your notes and are well rested and sitting in a comfortable chair in a slightly dimmed room with no distractions at all.

Think of someone you need to forgive so you may move on with your life—you may need to forgive yourself!

I use this in my live seminars with incredible results.

Repeat these words with power, love, conviction and peacefulness.

I FORGIVE YOU

I FORGIVE YOU

I FORGIVE YOU

I WILL ABSOLUTELY REFUSE TO LET YOU HAVE ANY POWER

OVER MYSELF,

MY LIFE,

MY FAMILY,

IN ANY MANNER WHATSOEVER.

I RELEASE MYSELF,

FROM YOU,

FOREVER.

NOW I AM IN CHARGE.

IT'S MY LIFE.

I CHOOSE HOW I RUN IT.

I CHOOSE HOW I LIVE IT.

I CHOOSE POWER.

I CHOOSE FAITH.

I CHOOSE LOVE.

I CHOOSE HAPPINESS.

I CHOOSE FAITH.

I CHOOSE HEALTH.

I CHOOSE WEALTH.

I CHOOSE STRENGTH.

I CHOOSE FREEDOM.

I CHOOSE LIFE.

I CHOOSE LOVE.

I CHOOSE TRANQUILITY.

I CHOOSE PEACE.

I CHOOSE SERENITY.

I CHOOSE BLISS.

I AM POWERFUL.

I AM FAITHFUL.

I AM LOVING.

I AM LOVED.

I AM TRULY LOVED.

I AM HAPPY.

I AM GOOD ENOUGH.

I AM ENOUGH.

I AM FORGIVING.

I AM FORGIVENESS.

I AM WEALTHY.

I AM HEALTHY.

I AM STRENGTH.

I AM FREE.

I AM LIFE.

I AM LOVE.

I AM TRANQUIL.

I AM PEACEFUL.

I AM SERENE.

I AM BLISSFUL.

I HAVE THE FAITH.

I HAVE THE HEALTH.

I HAVE THE WEALTH.

I HAVE THE STRENGTH.

I HAVE THE FREEDOM.

I HAVE THE LIFE.

I HAVE THE LOVE.

I HAVE THE TRANQUILITY.

I HAVE THE PEACE.

I HAVE THE SERENITY.

I HAVE THE BLISS.

I HAVE THE POWER.

I HAVE THE VISION.

I HAVE THE DESIRE.

I HAVE THE PASSION.

I HAVE THE CONVICTION.

I FORGIVE YOU.

I FORGIVE YOU.

I FORGIVE YOU.

I FORGIVE YOU.

I FORGIVE YOU.

I FORGIVE YOU.

I FORGIVE YOU.

I FORGIVE YOU.

I FORGIVE YOU.

I LOVE ME.

I LOVE ME.

I LOVE ME.

I LOVE ME.

I LOVE ME.

I LOVE ME.

Chapter 38

FULFILLMENT

If you have read this book thoroughly and performed the exercises then you will be feeling fulfilled but you may not know why!

No one teaches us how to reach fulfillment—the reason you are feeling fulfilled is because you have satisfied the 3 Pathways to Fulfillment—if you perform these three pathways then you will be filled with so much joy and happiness.

It is simple and profound.

1. **Growth** – you have to grow:
   a. Emotionally
   b. Spiritually
   c. Physically
   d. Mentally

2. **Give** – you have to give:
   a. Your time to others
   b. Your time to you
   c. Your energy to others
   d. Your energy to you
   e. Your love to others
   f. Your love to you
   g. Your forgiveness to others
   h. Your forgiveness to you
   i. Your service to others
   j. Your service to you
   k. Your love to others
   l. Your love to you
   m. Your compassion to others
   n. Your compassion to you
   o. To others
   p. To you
   q. Etc., etc,

3. **Gratitude** – have gratitude for everything and everybody

www.ImmediateHappiness.com

Chapter 39

UPDATES AND FURTHER INFORMATION

You now have the knowledge to completely change the way you live your life and to get the best results you must IMMERSE yourself in improving you. I use a system called AIM—which stands for ALWAYS IMPROVING MYSELF. If you apply that system you will, without fail, always be becoming a better person and all the riches of the world will come your way. Having great AIM will mean you will always be on target.

I urge you all to just use this simple system on a daily basis and the results will be compounded very quickly.

For further information on how to reach higher levels please go to my website where you will be able to access many updates, tools and products like my DVD set, blogs, videos, and inspiring content.

www.ImmediateHappiness.com

PART TWO

Chapter 40

POWERFUL QUOTES TO PONDER

This book has shown you that solutions are simple. Tools are easy to use and we just need to be conscious to remember that we are in charge and we choose. Here is a collection of some of my favorite quotes to help bring you into awareness.

"Pain is inevitable; suffering is optional." —*Author Unknown*

". . . all men make mistakes, but a good man yields when he knows his course is wrong, and repairs the evil. The only crime is pride."
—*Sophocles*

"An idea that is developed and put into action is more important than an idea that exists only as an idea." —*Buddha*

"Everything that irritates us about others can lead us to an understanding of ourselves." —*Carl Jung*

"An ounce of practice is worth more than tons of preaching."
—*Mohandas Gandhi*

"A man may die, nations may rise and fall, but an idea lives on."
—*John F. Kennedy*

"Faith is taking the first step even when you don't see the whole staircase." —*Martin Luther King, Jr.*

"Choose a job you love, and you will never have to work a day in your life. It is always the right time to do the right thing." —*Anil Gupta*

"Anyone can become angry—that is easy. But to be angry with the right person, to the right degree, at the right time, for the right purpose, and in the right way—this is not easy." —*Aristotle*

"If there is any Kindness I can show, or any good thing I can do to any fellow human being, let me do it now, and not defer or neglect it, as I shall not pass this way again." —*William Penn*

"Enjoying life is one of the best ways of lengthening it." —*Patrick McGrady*

"A life spent making mistakes is not only more honorable, but more useful than a life spent doing nothing." —*George Bernard Shaw*

"Holding on to anger is like grasping a hot coal with the intent of throwing it at someone else; you are the one who gets burned." —*Buddha*

"Being entirely honest with oneself is a good exercise." —*Sigmund Freud*

"Be the change that you want to see in the world." —*Mohandas Gandhi*

"Do not pray for easy lives. Pray to be stronger men." —*John F. Kennedy*

"If a man is called to be a street sweeper, he should sweep streets even as Michelangelo painted, or Beethoven composed music, or Shakespeare wrote poetry. He should sweep streets so well that all the hosts of heaven and earth will pause to say, here lived a great street sweeper who did his job well." —*Martin Luther King, Jr.*

One reason so few of us achieve what we truly want is that we never direct our focus; we never concentrate our power. Most people dabble their way through life, never deciding to master anything in particular." —*Anthony Robbins*

"It's kind of fun to do the impossible." —*Walt Disney*

"He who asks is a fool for five minutes, but he who does not ask remains a fool forever." —*Chinese Proverb*

"You can't blame gravity for falling in love." —*Albert Einstein*

"I'm a slow walker, but I never walk back." —*Abraham Lincoln*

"It's easy to make a buck. It's a lot tougher to make a difference." —*Tom Brokaw*

"I haven't failed. I've just found 10,000 ways that won't work." —*Thomas Edison*

"It's not whether you get knocked down, it's whether you get up." —*Vince Lombardi*

"When you come to the end of your rope, tie a knot and hang on." —*Franklin D. Roosevelt*

"A successful man is one who can lay a firm foundation with the bricks others have thrown at him." —*David Brinkley*

"Hitch your wagon to a star." —*Ralph Waldo Emerson*

"Always do whatever's next." —*George Carlin*

"Logic will get you from A to B. Imagination will take you everywhere." —*Albert Einstein*

"People must be taken as they are, and we should never try make them or ourselves better by quarreling with them." —*Edmund Burke*

"Have you ever noticed that anybody driving slower than you is an idiot, and anyone going faster than you is a maniac?" —*George Carlin*

"Married men live longer than single men. But married men are a lot more willing to die." —*Johnny Carson*

"There are only two ways to live your life. One is as though nothing is a miracle. The other is as though everything is a miracle." —*Albert Einstein*

"If you're quiet, you're not living. You've got to be noisy and colorful and lively." —*Mel Brooks*

"Be quick to learn and wise to know." —*George Burns*

"In wisdom gathered over time I have found that every expression is a form of exploration." —*Ansel Adams*

"Always desire to learn something useful." —*Sophocles*

"Always do your best. What you plant now, you will harvest later."
—*Og Mandino*

"Be miserable. Or motivate yourself. Whatever has to be done, it's always your choice." —*Wayne Dyer*

"Be gentle to all and stern with yourself." —*Saint Teresa of Avila*

"Do you want to know who you are? Don't Ask. Act! Action will delineate and define you." —*Thomas Jefferson*

"Either you run the day or the day runs you." —*Jim Rohn*

"Even if you fall on your face, you're still moving forward." —*Victor Kiam*

"Develop success from failures. Discouragement and failure are two of the surest stepping stones to success." —*Dale Carnegie*

"Diligence is the mother of good fortune." —*Benjamin Disraeli*

"Action is the foundational key to all success." —*Pablo Picasso*

"Beauty in things exists in the mind which contemplates them."
—*David Hume*

"A man's growth is seen in the successive choirs of his friends."
—*Ralph Waldo Emerson*

"Friends and good manners will carry you where money won't go."
—*Margaret Walker*

"Friendship…is not something you learn in school. But if you haven't learned the meaning of friendship, you really haven't learned anything." —*Muhammad Ali*

"A mistake is simply another way of doing things." —*Katharine Graham*

"A poem begins in delight and ends in wisdom." —*Robert Frost*

"A prudent question is one-half of wisdom." —*Francis Bacon*

"The reason I talk to myself is that I'm the only one whose answers I accept." —*George Carlin*

"Decide that you want it more than you are afraid of it." —*Bill Cosby*

"Action is the real measure of intelligence." —*Napoleon Hill*

"Be as smart as you can, but remember that it is always better to be wise than to be smart." —*Alan Alda*

"All men who have achieved great things have been great dreamers." —*Orison Swett Marden*

"A good marriage would be between a blind wife and a deaf husband." —*Michel de Montaigne*

"Do not hire a man who does your work for money, but him who does it for love of it." —*Henry David Thoreau*

"Deep experience is never peaceful." —*Henry James*

"It is during our darkest moments that we must focus to see the light." —*Aristotle Onassis*

"Continuous effort—not strength or intelligence—is the key to unlocking our potential." —*Winston Churchill*

"Ignorance is always afraid of change." —*Jawaharlal Nehru*

"It is health that is real wealth and not pieces of gold and silver." —*Mohandas Gandhi*

"I never see what has been done; I only see what remains to be done." —*Buddha*

"None but ourselves can free our minds." —*Bob Marley*

"All I am, or can be, I owe to my angel mother." —*Abraham Lincoln*

"Beware of little expenses. A small leak will sink a great ship." —*Benjamin Franklin*

"Love and compassion are necessities, not luxuries. Without them humanity cannot survive." —*Dalai Lama*

"I don't mind living in a man's world as long as I can be a woman in it." —*Marilyn Monroe*

"The hunger for love is much more difficult to remove than the hunger for bread." —*Mother Teresa*

"Never lend your car to anyone to whom you have given birth." —*Erma Bombeck*

"Age is an issue of mind over matter. If you don't mind, it doesn't matter." —*Mark Twain*

"Anyone who says he can see through women is missing a lot."
—*Groucho Marx*

"If it were not for hopes, the heart would break." —*Thomas Fuller*

"In a gentle way, you can shake the world." —*Gandhi*

"All life is an experiment. The more experiments you make the better." —*Ralph Waldo Emerson*

"Any idiot can face a crisis—it's day to day living that wears you out."
—*Anton Chekhov*

"Don't go around saying the world owes you a living. The world owes, you nothing. It was here first." —*Mark Twain*

"Every man dies. Not every man really lives." —*William Wallace*

"I love life because what more is there." —*Anthony Hopkins*

"Fall seven times and stand up eight." —*Japanese Proverb*

"It's hard to beat a person who never gives up." —*Babe Ruth*

"I never thought I didn't have a card to play." —*Jim Lovell*

"Never build your emotional life on the weaknesses of others."
—*George Santayana*

"We cannot always control our thoughts, but we can control our words, and repetition impresses the subconscious, and we are then master of the situation." —*Jane Fonda*

"When you go in search of honey you must expect to be stung by bees." —*Joseph Joubert*

"The noblest spirit is most strongly attracted by the love of glory." —*James Baldwin*

"Houston, Tranquility Base here. The Eagle has landed." —*Neil Armstrong*

"For the friendship of two, the patience of one is required." —*Indian Proverb*

If I knew it would be the last time
that I'd see you fall asleep,
I would tuck you in more tightly
and pray the Lord, your soul to keep.

If I knew it would be the last time
that I see you walk out the door,
I would give you a hug and kiss
and call you back for one more.

If I knew it would be the last time
I'd hear your voice lifted up in praise,
I would videotape each action and word,
so I could play them back day after day.

If I knew it would be the last time,
I could spare an extra minute or two
to stop and say "I love you,"
instead of assuming, you would *know* I do.

If I knew it would be the last time
I would be there to share your day,
well I'm sure you'll have so many more,
so I can let just this one slip away.

For surely there's always tomorrow
to make up for an oversight,
and we always get a second chance
to make everything right.

There will always be another day
to say "I love you"
And certainly there's another chance
to ask "Anything I can do?"

But just in case I might be wrong,
and today is all I get,
I'd like to say how much I love you
and I hope we never forget,
Tomorrow is not promised to anyone,
young or old alike,
And today may be the last chance
you get to hold your loved one tight.

So if you're waiting for tomorrow,
why not do it today?
For if tomorrow never comes,
you'll surely regret the day,
That you didn't take that extra time
for a smile, a hug, or a kiss
and you were too busy to grant someone,
what turned out to be their one last wish.

So hold your loved ones close today,
whisper in their ear,
Tell them how much you love them
and that you'll always hold them dear,

Take time to say "I'm sorry,"
"please forgive me," "thank you" or "it's okay".
And if tomorrow never comes,
you'll have no regrets about today.

—*Author Unknown*

www.ImmediateHappiness.com

Chapter 41

MEANINGFUL STORIES

A Tragedy or a Blessing

Years ago in Scotland, the Clark family had a dream. Clark and his wife worked and saved, making plans for their nine children and themselves to travel to the United States. It had taken years, but they had finally saved enough money and had gotten passports and reservations for the whole family on a new liner to the United States.

The entire family was filled with anticipation and excitement about their new life. However, seven days before their departure, a dog bit the youngest son. The doctor sewed up the boy but hung a yellow sheet on the Clarks' front door. Because of the possibility of rabies, they were being quarantined for fourteen days.

The family's dreams were dashed. They would not be able to make the trip to America as they had planned. The father, filled with disappointment and anger, stomped to the dock to watch the ship leave—without the Clark family. The father shed tears of disappointment and cursed both his son and God for their misfortune.

Five days later, the tragic news spread throughout Scotland—the mighty Titanic had sunk. The unsinkable ship had sunk, taking hundreds of lives with it. The Clark family was to have been on that ship, but because a dog had bitten the son, they were left behind in Scotland.

When Mr. Clark heard the news, he hugged his son and thanked him for saving the family. He thanked God for saving their lives and turning what he had felt was a tragedy into a blessing.

Although we may not always understand, all things happen for a reason.

Packing Parachutes

Charles Plumb, a US Navy Academy graduate, was a jet fighter pilot in Vietnam. After 75 combat missions, his plane was destroyed by a surface-to-air missile. Plumb ejected and parachuted into enemy hands. He was captured and spent the next six years in a Communist prison. He survived that ordeal and now lectures about lessons learned from that experience.

One day, when he and his wife were sitting in a restaurant, a man at another table came up and said, "You're Plumb! You flew jet fighters in Nam from the carrier, Kitty Hawk. You were shot down!" "How in the world did you know that?" asked Plumb. "Oh, I was the one who packed your parachute," the man replied. Plumb gasped in surprise and gratitude. The man smiled and said, "Yep, I guess it worked!" Plumb assured him, "It sure did work—if your chute hadn't worked, I wouldn't be here today."

Plumb couldn't sleep that night, thinking about the man who has packed his parachute. Plumb kept wondering what the man might have looked like in a Navy uniform. "I wondered how many times I might have passed him on the Kitty Hawk. I wondered how many times I might have seen him and not even said good morning, how are you or anything, because you see, I was a fighter pilot and he was just a sailor." Plumb thought of the many hours the sailor had spent on a long wooden table in the bowels of the ship carefully weaving the shrouds and folding the silks of each chute, holding in his hands the fate of someone he didn't know.

Now Plumb asks his audiences, "Who's packing your chute?" Everyone has someone who provides what they need to make it through the day. Plumb also points out that we all need many kinds of parachutes. We need mental, emotional and spiritual parachutes as well. While a prisoner of war, Plumb called on all of these supports before reaching

safety. His experience reminds us all to prepare ourselves to weather whatever storms lie ahead—and to recognize and appreciate all of those people who pack our parachutes everyday, for they are the ones who truly deserve the credit for our survival.

The Cross Room

The young man was at the end of his rope. Seeing no way out, he dropped to his knees in prayer. "Lord, I can't go on," he said. "I have too heavy a cross to bear." The Lord replied, "My son, if you can't bear its weight, just place your cross inside this room. Then, open that other door, and pick out any cross you wish."

The man was filled with relief. "Thank you, Lord," he sighed, and he did as he was told. Upon entering the other door, he saw many crosses, some so large the tops were not visible. Then he spotted a tiny cross leaning against a far wall. "I'd like that one, Lord," he whispered. And the Lord replied, "My son, that's the cross you just brought in."

Everybody Won

Last night was the last game for my eight-year-old son's soccer team. It was the final quarter. The score was two to one, my son's team in the lead. Parents shouted encouragement from the sidelines as the boys clashed on the field. With less than ten seconds remaining, the ball rolled in front of my son's teammate, one Mikey O'Donnel. With shouts of "Kick it!" echoing across the field, Mikey reared back and gave it everything he had.

All around me the crowd fell silent as the ball flew into the goal. Mikey O'Donnel had scored!

Mikey had scored all right, but in the wrong goal, ending the game in a tie. For a moment there was total silence. You see Mikey has Down's Syndrome and for him there is no such thing as a wrong goal. All goals were celebrated by a joyous hug from Mikey. He had even been known to hug the opposing players when they scored.

The silence was finally broken when Mikey, his face filled with joy, grabbed my son, hugged him and yelled, "I scored! I scored. Everybody won! Everybody won!"

For a moment I held my breath, not sure how my son would react. I need not have worried. I watched, through tears, as my son threw up his hand in the classic high-five salute and started chanting, "Way to go Mikey! Way to go Mikey!"

Within moments, both teams surrounded Mikey, joining in the chant and congratulating him on his goal. Later that night, when my daughter asked who had won, my son smiled and replied, "It was a tie. Everybody won!"

A Piece of Chalk

In our home it was natural to fear our father. Even our mother was afraid of him. As children, my sister and I thought every family was like that. Every family had an unpredictable dad who was impossible to please and a praying mama who was there to protect the children. We thought God planned it that way.

We were good children. Mama was always telling us we were, even if Daddy couldn't see it. Part of this was because we dared not do anything. We were quiet, timid children who rarely spoke, especially never when Daddy was home. People thought God had blessed Mama with the sweetest girls. She was always so proud.

Then came the day we found something new and fun to do. It wouldn't upset anyone; we'd never take the risk of doing that. We discovered we could draw pictures with chalk on our wooden front door, and it would rub right off. We could have lots of fun, so we set to work drawing and making lots of pretty pictures all over it. We had a great time. It surprised us to see how talented we were. We decided to finish our masterpiece, knowing Mama would just love it. She would want all her friends to come and see it, and maybe they would want us to do their doors, too.

The praise we expected did not come. Instead of seeing the obvious beauty in our work, all Mama could see was the time and effort she would need to clean it off. She was mad. We did not understand why, but we knew all about anger, and we were in big trouble!

Off we ran to find a place to hide. In our wooded yard it was not hard for two small children to find safety. Together, we huddled behind a tree and did not move. Soon we heard the frightened voices of Mom and our neighbors calling out to us. Still we did not budge. They were afraid we had run away or drowned in the pond out back. We were afraid of being found.

The sun set, and it began to get dark. Those around us became more anxious, and we became more frightened. Time was slipping by, and the longer we hid there, the harder it was to come out. Mom was, by now, convinced something awful had happened to us, and she resorted to calling the police. We could hear all the voices drawn together in a group. Then the search was on again, this time with strong male voices overpowering the others. If we were frightened before, now we were terrified!

As we clung together in the dark, we became aware of yet another voice, one we instantly recognized with horror: our daddy. But there was something strangely different about it. In it we heard something we had never heard before: fear, agony and despair. We couldn't put a name to it then, but that's what it was. Then came his prayers, tears and prayers intermingled together.

Was that our daddy on his knees pleading with God? Our daddy with tears running down his face, promising God that he would give his life to him if he would safely return his girls?

Nothing in our lives had prepared us for this kind of shock. Neither of us remembers making a decision to come out. We were drawn to him like a magnet, our fears dissolving into the forest. We don't know yet if we actually took steps or if God somehow moved us out and into Daddy's arms. What we do remember are those strong, loving arms holding us and crying, hugging us like we were precious.

Things were different after that. We had a new daddy. It was like the old one was buried that day in the forest. God had taken him and replaced him with another, one who loved us and was ever thankful for us.

Mama always told us that God was a God of miracles. I guess she was right. He changed our whole family with a piece of chalk.

Kyle

One day, when I was a freshman in high school, I saw a kid from my class was walking home from school. His name was Kyle. It looked like he was carrying all of his books. I thought to myself, "Why would anyone bring home all his books on a Friday? He must really be a nerd." I had quite a weekend planned (parties and a football game with my friends tomorrow afternoon), so I shrugged my shoulders and went on.

As I was walking, I saw a bunch of kids running toward him. They ran at him, knocking all his books out of his arms and tripping him so he landed in the dirt. His glasses went flying, and I saw them land in the grass about ten feet from him. He looked up and I saw this terrible sadness in his eyes. My heart went out to him. So, I jogged over to him and as he crawled around looking for his glasses, and I saw a tear in his eye.

As I handed him his glasses, I said, "Those guys are jerks. They really should get lives." He looked at me and said, "Hey thanks!" There was a big smile on his face. It was one of those smiles that showed real gratitude. I helped him pick up his books, and asked him where he lived. As it turned out, he lived near me, so I asked him why I had never seen him before. He said he had gone to private school before now. I would have never hung out with a private school kid before. We talked all the way home, and I carried his books. He turned out to be a pretty cool kid. I asked him if he wanted to play football on Saturday with me and my friends. He said yes. We hung all weekend and the more I got to know Kyle, the more I liked him, and my friends thought the same of him.

Monday morning came, and there was Kyle with the huge stack of books again. I stopped him and said, "Boy, you are gonna really build some serious muscles with this pile of books everyday!" He just

laughed and handed me half the books. Over the next four years, Kyle and I became best friends. When we were seniors, we began to think about college. Kyle decided on Georgetown, and I was going to Duke. I knew that we would always be friends, that the miles would never be a problem. He was going to be a doctor, and I was going for business on a football scholarship.

Kyle was valedictorian of our class. I teased him all the time about being nerd. He had to prepare a speech for graduation. I was so glad it wasn't me having to get up there and speak.

Graduation day, I saw Kyle. He looked great. He was one of those guys that really found himself during high school. He filled out and actually looked good in glasses. He had more dates than I had and all the girls loved him. Boy, sometimes I was jealous. Today was one of those days. I could see that he was nervous about his speech. So, I smacked him on the back and said, "Hey, big guy, you'll be great!" He looked at me with one of those looks (the really grateful one) and smiled. "Thanks," he said.

As he started his speech, he cleared his throat, and began. "Graduation is a time to thank those who helped you make it through those tough years. Your parents, your teachers, your siblings, maybe a coach . . . but mostly your friends. I am here to tell all of you that being a friend to someone is the best gift you can give them. I am going to tell you a story."

I just looked at my friend with disbelief as he told the story of the first day we met. He had planned to kill himself over the weekend. He talked of how he had cleaned out his locker so his Mom wouldn't have to do it later and was carrying his stuff home. He looked hard at me and gave me a little smile. "Thankfully, I was saved. My friend saved me from doing the unspeakable. "I heard the gasp go through the crowd as this handsome, popular boy told us all about his weakest moment. I saw his mom and dad looking at me and smiling that same grateful smile. Not until that moment did I realize it's depth.

Never underestimate the power of your actions. With one small gesture you can change a person's life. For better or for worse. God puts us all in each other's lives to impact one another in some way. Look for God in others.

Resentment

Two men, both seriously ill, occupied the same hospital room. One man was allowed to sit up in his bed for an hour a day to drain the fluids from his lungs. His bed was next to the room's only window. The other man had to spend all his time flat on his back.

The men talked for hours on end. They spoke of their wives and families, their homes, their jobs, their involvement in the military service, where they had been on vacation. And every afternoon when the man in the bed next to the window could sit up, he would pass the time by describing to his roommate all the things he could see outside the window.

The man in the other bed would live for those one-hour periods where his world would be broadened and enlivened by all the activity and color of the outside world. The window overlooked a park with a lovely lake, the man had said. Ducks and swans played on the water while children sailed their model boats. Lovers walked arm in arm amid flowers of every color of the rainbow. Grand old trees graced the landscape, and a fine view of the city skyline could be seen in the distance. As the man by the window described all this in exquisite detail, the man on the other side of the room would close his eyes and imagine the picturesque scene.

One warm afternoon the man by the window described a parade passing by. Although the other man could not hear the band, he could see it in his mind's eye as the gentleman by the window portrayed it with descriptive words. Unexpectedly, an alien thought entered his head: Why should he have all the pleasure of seeing everything while I never get to see anything? It didn't seem fair. As the thought fermented, the man felt ashamed at first. But as the days passed and he missed seeing more sights, his envy eroded into resentment and soon turned him sour. He began to brood and found himself unable to sleep. He should be by that window—and that thought now controlled his life . . .

Late one night, as he lay staring at the ceiling, the man by the window began to cough. He was choking on the fluid in his lungs. The other man watched in the dimly lit room as the struggling man by the window groped for the button to call for help. Listening from across the room, he never moved, never pushed his own button which would have brought the nurse running. In less than five minutes, the coughing and choking stopped, along with the sound of breathing. Now, there was only silence—deathly silence.

The following morning, the day nurse arrived to bring water for their baths. When she found the lifeless body of the man by the window, she was saddened and called the hospital attendant to take it away—no words, no fuss. As soon as it seemed appropriate, the man asked if he could be moved next to the window. The nurse was happy to make the switch and after making sure he was comfortable, she left him alone.

Slowly, painfully, he propped himself up on one elbow to take his first look. Finally, he would have the joy of seeing it all himself. He strained to slowly turn to look out the window beside the bed. It faced a blank wall.

Just a Mom

A woman, renewing her driver's license at the County Clerk's office, was asked by the woman recorder to state her occupation.

She hesitated, uncertain how to classify herself.

"What I mean is," explained the recorder, "do you have a job or are you just a . . . ?"

"Of course I have a job," snapped the woman.

"I'm a mom."

"We don't list 'mom' as an occupation, 'housewife' covers it," said the recorder emphatically.

I forgot all about her story until one day I found myself in the same situation, this time at our own Town Hall. The clerk was obviously a career woman, poised, efficient, and possessed of a high sounding title

like, "Official Interrogator" or "Town Registrar."

"What is your occupation?" she probed.

What made me say it? I do not know. The words simply popped out. "I'm a Research Associate in the field of Child Development and Human Relations."

The clerk paused, ball-point pen frozen in midair and looked up as though she had not heard right.

I repeated the title slowly emphasizing the most significant words. Then I stared with wonder as my pronouncement was written, in bold, black ink on the official questionnaire.

"Might I ask," said the clerk with new interest, "just what you do in your field?"

Coolly, without any trace of fluster in my voice, I heard myself reply, "I have a continuing program of research, (what mother doesn't) in the laboratory and in the field, (normally I would have said indoors and out). I'm working for my Masters, (first the Lord and then the whole family) and already have four credits (all daughters). Of course, the job is one of the most demanding in the humanities, (any mother care to disagree?) and I often work 14 hours a day, (24 is more like it). But the job is more challenging than most run-of-the-mill careers and the rewards are more of a satisfaction rather than just money."

There was an increasing note of respect in the clerk's voice as she completed the form, stood up, and personally ushered me to the door.

As I drove into our driveway, buoyed up by my glamorous new career, I was greeted by my lab assistants—ages 13, 7, and 3. Upstairs I could hear our new experimental model, (a 6-month-old baby) in the child development program, testing out a new vocal pattern.

I felt I had scored a beat on bureaucracy! And I had gone on the official records as someone more distinguished and indispensable to mankind than "just another mom."

Serious Business

Let me take you back a couple years. Come with me as we relearn a lesson; one that has stuck with me, in my present memory, and inspires me yet. I don't remember exact conversation, but bear with me as I supply something that would sound normal.

We walk into Elida Road Hardware. An old fashioned hardware store. No automatic door, not a computer in the building. Nothing unusual about the day, or the fact that we go to that store. It is one that I go to fairly often. As we enter the door, two sounds greet us. The sleigh bells of yesteryear, the ones that make that sweet, peaceful tinkle as we open the door. The other sound is the electronic beeper that alerts Andy of our presence.

"Good afternoon, Ryan," comes the cheerful acknowledgment. Andy Bianco is a very friendly sort of proprietor. He is of medium build and height, we'll say about 50, and the smile on his face welcomes us.

We walk across the old wood floor—destitute of stain or varnish, and worn smooth—with its squeaky spots, and uneven joints. Andy asks us what he can help us with. I tell him we are looking for a spring. He very patiently replies "I carry lots of springs, you're going to need to be more specific."

"Beats me what they're called; just a spring for an old-fashioned screen door."

"That's it. A screen door spring. Right down there." We turn to where he is pointing, and sure enough, there they are. Andy knows his store, and his products. That's why I come here instead of Meijer. The service can't be beat. The price, Yes. But service and satisfaction; no.

I pick up one and follow him to the counter. A keg of peanuts sits beside the counter, and beside it, another for the hulls. Let me know when Lowe's does that. Covering the counter is a piece of Plexiglas, and under it, all manner of business cards.

"Hey got a card? Put one under here. Free advertising space."

"Thanks Andy, but I already have one. See, over here."

"Well, I'll be; you do."

He figures up the price, doing the math in his head. "$1.88, with Uncle Sam's share comes to $1.99"

"Put it on Pop's account."

He nods and smiles, remembering that this is the third item this week that received that verdict.

"Good ole' Pop's account." He chuckles. "I don't know what you boys would do without Pop's account!"

He hands me the ticket and as I sign it I ask rhetorically, "You really trust my signature?"

His reply startles, yet gladdens me. "When I can't trust Jerry Hoover's boys; I can't trust nobody!"

We leave, and the brain immediately starts to forget things, in order of importance. But what Andy Bianco said that day, rang in my ears. And it rings in my ears today. That's a tall order to live up to. It's a high standard of integrity. My father made a reputation for that name, and I get to enjoy the benefits thereof. But by the same token, I must maintain that reputation. And that's serious business.

Who I Am Makes a Difference

A teacher in New York decided to honor each of her seniors in High School by telling them the difference each of them had made. She called each student to the front of the class, one at a time. First, she told each of them how they had made a difference to her, and the class. Then she presented each of them with a blue ribbon, imprinted with gold letters, which read, "Who I Am Makes a Difference."

Afterwards, the teacher decided to do a class project, to see what kind of impact recognition would have on a community. She gave each student three more blue ribbons, and instructed them to go out and spread this acknowledgment ceremony. Then they were to follow up on the results, see who honored whom, and report to the class in about a week.

One of the boys in the class went to a junior executive in a nearby company, and honored him for helping him with his career planning.

He gave him a blue ribbon, and put it on his shirt.

Then he gave him two extra ribbons and said, "We're doing a class project on recognition, and we'd like for you to go out, find someone to honor, and give them a blue ribbon. Then give them this extra blue ribbon, so they can acknowledge a third person, to keep this ceremony going. Then please get back to me and tell me what happened."

Later that day, the junior executive went in to see his boss, who had a reputation of being kind of a grouchy fellow. He told him that he deeply admired him for being a creative genius.

The boss seemed very surprised. The junior executive asked him if he would accept the gift of the blue ribbon, and give him permission to put it on him.

His boss said, "Well, sure."

The junior executive took one of the blue ribbons and placed it right on his boss's jacket, above his heart. And then he asked, offering him the last ribbon, "Would you take this extra ribbon, and pass it on by honoring somebody else. The teenager who gave me these is doing a school project, and we want to keep this ribbon ceremony going and see how it affects people."

That night, the boss came home and sat down with his 14-year-old son. He said, "The most incredible thing happened to me today. I was in my office, and one of my employees came in and told me he admired me, and gave me a blue ribbon for being a creative genius. Imagine! He thinks I am a creative genius! Then he put a blue ribbon on me that says, 'Who I Am Makes a Difference.' He gave me an extra ribbon and asked me to find somebody else to honor. As I was driving home tonight, I started thinking about who I would honor with this ribbon, and I thought about you. I want to honor you. My days are hectic and when I come home, I don't pay a lot of attention to you. I yell at you for not getting good enough grades and for your messy bedroom. Somehow, tonight, I just wanted to sit here and, well, just let you know that you do make a difference to me. Besides your mother, you are the most important person in my life. You're a great kid, and I love you!"

The startled boy started to sob and sob, and he couldn't stop crying. His whole body shook. He looked up at his father and said through his tears, "Dad, earlier tonight I sat in my room and wrote a letter to you and Mom, explaining why I had took my life, and I asked you to forgive me. I was going to commit suicide tonight after you were asleep. I just didn't think that you cared at all. The letter is upstairs. I don't think I'll need it after all."

Running in the Rain

She had been shopping with her mom in Wal-Mart. She must have been 6 years old, this beautiful red haired, freckle faced image of innocence. It was pouring outside. The kind of rain that gushes over the top of rain gutters, so much in a hurry to hit the earth it has no time to flow down the spout. We all stood there under the awning and just inside the door of the Wal-Mart. We waited, some patiently, others irritated because nature messed up their hurried day. I am always mesmerized by rainfall. I got lost in the sound and sight of the heavens washing away the dirt and dust of the world. Memories were a welcome reprieve from the worries of my day.

Her voice was so sweet as it broke the hypnotic trance we were all caught in, "Mom, let's run through the rain," she said. "What?" Mom asked. "Let's run through the rain!" She repeated. "No, honey. We'll wait until it slows down a bit," Mom replied. This young child waited about another minute and repeated: "Mom, let's run through the rain." "We'll get soaked if we do," Mom said. "No, we won't, Mom. That's not what you said this morning," the young girl said as she tugged at her Mom's arm.

"This morning? When did I say we could run through the rain and not get wet?" "Don't you remember? When you were talking to Daddy about his cancer, you said, 'If God can get us through this, he can get us through anything!'" The entire crowd stopped dead silent. I swear you couldn't hear anything but the rain. We all stood silently. No one came or left in the next few minutes.

Mom paused and thought for a moment about what she would say. Now some would laugh it off and scold her for being silly. Some might even ignore what was said. But this was a moment of affirmation in a young child's life. A time when innocent trust can be nurtured so that it will bloom into faith. "Honey, you are absolutely right. Let's run through the rain. If GOD let's us get wet, well maybe we just needed washing," Mom said. Then off they ran. We all stood watching, smiling and laughing as they darted past the cars and yes, through the puddles. They held their shopping bags over their heads just in case. They got soaked. But they were followed by a few who screamed and laughed like children all the way to their cars. And yes, I did. I ran. I got wet. I needed washing.

Circumstances or people can take away your material possessions, they can take away your money, and they can take away your health. But no one can ever take away your precious memories . . . So, don't forget to make time and take the opportunities to make memories every day.

Rocks

One day, an expert in time management was speaking to a group of business students and, to drive home a point, used an illustration those students will never forget.

As he stood in front of the group of high-powered overachievers he said, "Okay, time for a quiz" and he pulled out a one-gallon, wide-mouth Mason jar and set it on the table in front of him. He also produced about a dozen fist-sized rocks and carefully placed them, one at a time, into the jar. When the jar was filled to the top and no more rocks would fit inside, he asked, "Is this jar full?"

Everyone in the class yelled, "Yes."

The time management expert replied, "Really?" He reached under the table and pulled out a bucket of gravel. He dumped some gravel in and shook the jar causing pieces of gravel to work themselves down into the spaces between the big rocks. He then asked the group once more, "Is the jar full?"

By this time the class was on to him. "Probably not," one of them answered. "Good!" he replied. He reached under the table and brought out a bucket of sand. He started dumping the sand in the jar and it went into all of the spaces left between the rocks and the gravel. Once more he asked the question, "Is this jar full?"

"No!" the class shouted. Once again he said, Good." Then he grabbed a pitcher of water and began to pour it in until the jar was filled to the brim. Then he looked at the class and asked, "What is the point of this illustration?" One eager beaver raised his hand and said, "The point is, no matter how full your schedule is, if you try really hard you can always fit some more things in it!"

"No," the speaker replied, "that's not the point. The truth this illustration teaches us is if you don't put the big rocks in first, you'll never get them in at all. What are the 'big rocks' in your life, time with your loved ones, your faith, your education, your dreams, a worthy cause, teaching or mentoring others? Remember to put these BIG ROCKS in first or you'll never get them in at all.

So, tonight, or in the morning, when you are reflecting on this short story, ask yourself this question: What are the "big rocks" in my life? Then, put those in your jar first.

The Red Marbles

I was at the corner grocery store buying some early potatoes. I noticed a small boy, delicate of bone and feature, ragged but clean, hungrily apprising a basket of freshly picked green peas.

I paid for my potatoes but was also drawn to the display of fresh green peas. I am a pushover for creamed peas and new potatoes. Pondering the peas, I couldn't help overhearing the conversation between Mr. Miller (the store owner) and the ragged boy next to me.

"Hello Barry, how are you today?"

"H'lo, Mr. Miller. Fine, thank ya. Jus' admirin' them peas. They sure look good."

"They are good, Barry. How's your ma?"

"Fine. Gittin' stronger alla' time."

"Good. Anything I can help you with?"

"No, Sir. Jus' admirin' them peas."

"Would you like to take some home?" asked Mr. Miller.

"No, Sir. Got nuthin' to pay for 'em with."

"Well, what have you to trade me for some of those peas?"

"All I got's my prize marble here."

"Is that right? Let me see it," said Miller.

"Here 'tis. She's a dandy."

"I can see that. Hmmmmm, only thing is this one is blue and I sort of go for red. Do you have a red one like this at home?" the store owner asked.

"Not zackley but almost."

"Tell you what. Take this sack of peas home with you and next trip this way let me look at that red marble," Mr. Miller told the boy.

"Sure will. Thanks Mr. Miller."

Mrs. Miller, who had been standing nearby, came over to help me. With a smile she said, "There are two other boys like him in our community, all three are in very poor circumstances. Jim just loves to bargain with them for peas, apples, tomatoes, or whatever. When they come back with their red marbles, and they always do, he decides he doesn't like red after all and he sends them home with a bag of produce for a green marble or an orange one, when they come on their next trip to the store."

I left the store smiling to myself, impressed with this man. A short time later I moved to Colorado, but I never forgot the story of this man, the boys, and their bartering for marbles.

Several years went by, each more rapid than the previous one. Just recently I had occasion to visit some old friends in that Idaho community and while I was there learned that Mr. Miller had died. They were having his visitation that evening and knowing my friends wanted to go, I agreed to accompany them. Upon arrival at the mortuary we fell into line to meet the relatives of the deceased and to offer whatever

words of comfort we could.

Ahead of us in line were three young men. One was in an army uniform and the other two wore nice haircuts, dark suits and white shirts . . . all very professional looking. They approached Mrs. Miller, standing composed and smiling by her husband's casket. Each of the young men hugged her, kissed her on the cheek, spoke briefly with her and moved on to the casket.

Her misty light blue eyes followed them as, one by one; each young man stopped briefly and placed his own warm hand over the cold pale hand in the casket. Each left the mortuary awkwardly, wiping his eyes.

Our turn came to meet Mrs. Miller. I told her who I was and re-minded her of the story from those many years ago and what she had told me about her husband's bartering for marbles. With her eyes glistening, she took my hand and led me to the casket.

"Those three young men who just left were the boys I told you about. They just told me how they appreciated the things Jim "traded" them. Now, at last, when Jim could not change his mind about color or size . . . they came to pay their debt."

"We've never had a great deal of the wealth of this world," she confided, "but right now, Jim would consider himself the richest man in Idaho."

With loving gentleness she lifted the lifeless fingers of her deceased husband. Resting underneath were three exquisitely shined red marbles.

I Knew You Would Come

Horror gripped the heart of the World War I soldier as he saw his life-long friend fall in battle. Caught in a trench with continuous gunfire whizzing over his head, the soldier asked his lieutenant if he might go out into the "no man's land" between the trenches to bring his fallen comrade back.

"You can go," said the lieutenant, "but I don't think it will be worth it. Your friend is probably dead and you may throw your life away." The lieutenant's advice didn't matter, and the soldier went anyway.

Miraculously he managed to reach his friend, hoist him onto his

shoulder and bring him back to their company's trench. As the two of them tumbled in together to the bottom of the trench, the officer checked the wounded soldier, and then looked kindly at his friend.

"I told you it wouldn't be worth it," he said. "Your friend is dead and you are mortally wounded."

"It was worth it, though, sir," said the soldier.

"What do you mean; worth it?" responded the Lieutenant. "Your friend is dead."

"YES, Sir" the private answered. "But it was worth it because when I got to him, he was still alive and I had the satisfaction of hearing him saying, "JIM......, I KNEW YOU'D COME."

Two Chipmunks

Two chipmunks, Chipper and Bud, were best friends. They lived in a forest of plenty in which oak trees were so tall; they seemed to reach into the blue skies and they dropped a plentiful supply of nuts, in all but the coldest months of winter.

During the summer, the sun was warm and bright and the meadow was covered in flowers whose pedals bloomed in bright reds and purples and golden yellows.

Chipper and Bud frolicked together, exploring all that nature had to offer as they climbed the trees and smelled the perfumed scented flowers and joyfully munched on a wide variety of acorns and other nuts.

But as time passed, Bud began eating more nuts and climbed less as he began waddling through the meadow, the increasing size of his tummy slowing him down. And he was often winded as he tried to keep up with Chipper.

"You go ahead," Bud would say to Chipper. "I'll catch up later." Until after awhile, Bud spent most his day laying in the shade cast by a giant oak tree, and eating all the acorns in his reach.

"You've got to get in shape," Chipper would say to his best friend. "This isn't healthy for you." But Bud would ignore the advice, as his girth continued to grow.

Then one day, a sharp eyed hawk with a razor sharp beak and a six foot wingspan flew overhead looking for an easy meal. It didn't take him long to spot Bud.

"Run!" yelled Chipper in desperation, as he saw the hawk begin to dive down. "Run as fast as you can!" But it was too late.

Bud tried to run but he was far too slow. As the hawk swiftly swooped down his claws reached out for Bud. In just that instant, Bud stumbled and landed in a gopher hole. It saved his life.

As the hawk flew off in search of other prey, Chipper helped Bud out of the hole. Gasping for air and trembling from fright, it was several minutes before Bud could speak.

"Being in poor condition," said Chipper, "nearly cost you your life." Before responding Bud closed his eyes and tried to calm himself, his heart pounding so hard, it echoed in his ears. "I know," he gasped.

"Starting now," Bud said, "I'm going to eat less and exercise more. I never felt good about myself with a big tummy, and I've missed all the fun times we used to have together."

Chipper nuzzled his friend. "That's the spirit Bud," he said with a warm assuring smile. "It's good to have you back again, and thank goodness we get another chance. You will find life much more rewarding and the acorns you do eat will taste sweeter."

At times, most of us have had Bud's problem. But with a little care we can solve it and reap the rewards.

Three Stringed Violin

On Nov. 18, 1995, Itzhak Perlman, the violinist, came on stage to give a concert at Avery Fisher Hall at Lincoln Center in New York City.

If you have ever been to a Perlman concert, you know that getting on stage is no small achievement for him. He was stricken with polio as a child, and so he has braces on both legs and walks with the aid of two crutches. To see him walk across the stage one step at a time, painfully and slowly, is an awesome sight.

He walks painfully, yet majestically, until he reaches his chair. Then

he sits down, slowly, puts his crutches on the floor, undoes the clasps on his legs, tucks one foot back and extends the other foot forward. Then he bends down and picks up the violin, puts it under his chin, nods to the conductor and proceeds to play.

By now, the audience is used to this ritual. They sit quietly while he makes his way across the stage to his chair. They remain reverently silent while he undoes the clasps on his legs. They wait until he is ready to play.

But this time, something went wrong. Just as he finished the first few bars, one of the strings on his violin broke. You could hear it snap—it went off like gunfire across the room. There was no mistaking what that sound meant. There was no mistaking what he had to do.

We figured that he would have to get up, put on the clasps again, pick up the crutches and limp his way off stage—to either find another violin or else find another string for this one. But he didn't. Instead, he waited a moment, closed his eyes and then signaled the conductor to begin again.

The orchestra began, and he played from where he had left off. And he played with such passion and such power and such purity as they had never heard before.

Of course, anyone knows that it is impossible to play a symphonic work with just three strings. I know that, and you know that, but that night Itzhak Perlman refused to know that.

You could see him modulating, changing, re-composing the piece in his head. At one point, it sounded like he was de-tuning the strings to get new sounds from them that they had never made before.

When he finished, there was an awesome silence in the room. And then people rose and cheered. There was an extraordinary outburst of applause from every corner of the auditorium. We were all on our feet, screaming and cheering, doing everything we could to show how much we appreciated what he had done.

He smiled, wiped the sweat from this brow, raised his bow to quiet us, and then he said—not boastfully, but in a quiet, pensive, reverent tone—"You know, sometimes it is the artist's task to find out how much

music you can still make with what you have left."

What a powerful line that is. It has stayed in my mind ever since I heard it. And who knows? Perhaps that is the definition of life—not just for artists but for all of us.

Here is a man who has prepared all his life to make music on a violin of four strings, who, all of a sudden, in the middle of a concert, finds himself with only three strings; so he makes music with three strings, and the music he made that night with just three strings was more beautiful, more sacred, more memorable, than any that he had ever made before, when he had four strings.

So, perhaps our task in this shaky, fast-changing, bewildering world in which we live is to make music, at first with all that we have, and then, when that is no longer possible, to make music with what we have left.

All the Time in the World . . .

While at the park one day, a woman sat down next to a man on a bench near a playground. "That's my son over there," she said, pointing to a little boy in a red sweater who was gliding down the slide. "He's a fine looking boy," the man said.

"That's my son on the swing in the blue sweater." Then, looking at his watch, he called to his son. "What do you say we go, Todd?" Todd pleaded, "Just five more minutes, Dad. Please? Just five more minutes." The man nodded and Todd continued to swing to his heart's content.

Minutes passed and the father stood and called again to his son. "Time to go now?" Again Todd pleaded, "Five more minutes, Dad. Just five more minutes." The man smiled and said, "O.K."

"My, you certainly are a patient father," the woman responded.

The man smiled and then said, "My older son Tommy was killed by a drunk driver last year while he was riding his bike near here. I never spent much time with Tommy and now I'd give anything for just five more minutes with him. I've vowed not to make the same mistake with Todd. He thinks he has five more minutes to swing. The truth is . . . I get five more minutes to watch him play."

An Angel

An Angel wrote: Many people will walk in and out of your life, but only true friends will leave footprints in your heart.

To handle yourself, use your head; To handle others, use your heart.

Anger is only one letter short of danger.

If someone betrays you once, it's his fault; if he betrays you twice, it's your fault.

Great minds discuss ideas; Average minds discuss events; Small minds discuss people.

God gives every bird it's food, but He does not throw it into it's nest.

He who loses money, loses much; He who loses a friend, loses more; He who loses faith, loses all.

Beautiful young people are acts of nature, but beautiful old people are works of art.

Learn from the mistakes of others. You can't live long enough to make them all yourself.

The tongue weighs practically nothing, but so few people can hold it.

Choose How to Start Your Day

Jerry is the kind of guy you love to hate. He is always in a good mood and always has something positive to say. When someone would ask him how he was doing, he would reply, "If I were any better, I would be twins!" He was a unique manager because he had several waiters who had followed him around from restaurant to restaurant.

The reason the waiters followed Jerry was because of his attitude. He was a natural motivator. If an employee was having a bad day, Jerry was there telling the employee how to look on the positive side of the situation.

Seeing this style really made me curious, so one day I went up to Jerry and asked him, I don't get it! You can't be a positive person all of the time. How do you do it?" Jerry replied, "Each morning I wake up and say to myself, Jerry, you have two choices today. You can choose to be in a good mood or you can choose to be in a bad mood.

I choose to be in a good mood. Each time something bad happens, I can choose to be a victim or I can choose to learn from it. I choose to learn from it. Every time someone comes to me complaining, I can choose to accept their complaining or I can point out the positive side of life. I choose the positive side of life.

"Yeah, right, it's not that easy," I protested. "Yes, it is," Jerry said. "Life is all about choices. When you cut away all the junk, every situation is a choice. You choose how you react to situations. You choose how people will affect your mood. You choose to be in a good mood or bad mood. The bottom line: It's your choice how you live life."

I reflected on what Jerry said. Soon thereafter, I left the restaurant industry to start my own business. We lost touch, but I often thought about him when I made a choice about life instead of reacting to it.

Several years later, I heard that Jerry did something you are never supposed to do in a restaurant business: he left the back door open one morning and was held up at gun point by three armed robbers. While trying to open the safe, his hand, shaking from nervousness, slipped off the combination. The robbers panicked and shot him. Luckily, Jerry was found relatively quickly and rushed to the local trauma center. After 18 hours of surgery and weeks of intensive care, Jerry was released from the hospital with fragments of the bullets still in his body.

I saw Jerry about six months after the accident. When I asked him how he was, he replied, "If I were any better, I'd be twins. Wanna see my scars?" I declined to see his wounds, but did ask him what had gone through his mind as the robbery took place. "The first thing that went through my mind was that I should have locked the back door," Jerry replied. "Then, as I lay on the floor, I remembered that I had two choices: I could choose to live or I could choose to die. I chose to live."

"Weren't you scared? Did you lose consciousness?" I asked. Jerry continued, ". . . the paramedics were great. They kept telling me I was going to be fine. But when they wheeled me into the ER and I saw the expressions on the faces of the doctors and nurses, I got really scared. In their eyes, I read 'he's a dead man.' I knew I needed to take action."

"What did you do?" I asked.

"Well, there was a big burly nurse shouting questions at me," said Jerry. "She asked if I was allergic to anything. 'Yes,' I replied. The doctors and nurses stopped working as they waited for my reply. I took a deep breath and yelled, 'Bullets!' Over their laughter, I told them, 'I am choosing to live. Operate on me as if I am alive, not dead.'"

Jerry lived thanks to the skill of his doctors, but also because of his amazing attitude. I learned from him that every day we have the choice to live fully. Attitude, after all, is everything.

This is Good

An old story is told of a king in Africa who had a close friend with whom he grew up. The friend had a habit of looking at every situation that ever occurred in his life (positive or negative) and remarking, "This is good!"

One day the king and his friend were out on a hunting expedition. The friend would load and prepare the guns for the king. The friend had apparently done something wrong in preparing one of the guns, for after taking the gun from his friend, the king fired it and his thumb was blown off.

Examining the situation the friend remarked as usual, "This is good!" To which the king replied, "No, this is NOT good!" and proceeded to send his friend to jail.

About a year later, the king was hunting in an area that he should have known to stay clear of. Cannibals captured him and took him to their village. They tied his hands, stacked some wood, set up a stake and bound him to the stake. As they came near to set fire to the wood, they noticed that the king was missing a thumb. Being superstitious, they never ate anyone that was less than whole. So untying the king, they sent him on his way.

As he returned home, he was reminded of the event that had taken his thumb and felt remorse for his treatment of his friend. He went immediately to the jail to speak with his friend. "You were right," he

said, "it was good that my thumb was blown off."

And he proceeded to tell the friend all that had just happened. "And so I am very sorry for sending you to jail for so long. It was bad for me to do this." "No," his friend replied, "This is good!" "What do you mean, 'This is good'? How could it be good that I sent my friend to jail for a year?"

"If I had NOT been in jail, I would have been with you."

Starfish

While walking along a beach, an elderly gentleman saw someone in the distance leaning down, picking something up and throwing it back into the ocean. As he got closer, he noticed that the figure was that of a young man, picking up starfish one by one and tossing each one gently back into the water.

The old man smiled, and said, "I must ask, then, why are you throwing starfish into the ocean?"

To this, the young man replied, "The sun is up and the tide is going out. If I don't throw them in, they'll die."

Upon hearing this, the elderly observer commented, "But young man, do you not realize that there are miles and miles of beach and there are starfish all along every mile? You can't possibly make a difference!"

The young man listened politely. Then he bent down, picked up another starfish, threw it back into the ocean past the breaking waves and said, "It made a difference for that one."

Chapter 42

NAMASTE

The greatness inside me honors
the greatness inside you.
The divinity inside me honors
the divinity inside you.
The love inside me honors
the love inside you.

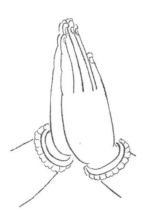

I invite you to visit me at *www.ImmediateHappiness.com*

.

Made in the USA
Columbia, SC
29 May 2017